Wh

Jewelle Taylor Gibbs, Ph.D.
Author of *Race and Justice*

Susie Ludlow's book about her Virginia roots offers the reader a multi-layered and moving account of one prominent African American family's heroic 300-year struggle to overcome the challenges of miscegenation, racism, economic hardship and educational segregation. The author provides valuable insights into the development of the black middle class, the conflicts over color and class within the black community, and the successful strategies of social mobility, preserving family heritage, and maintaining personal self-esteem within the context of a dominant white society.

Courtland Milloy
Columnist, *The Washington Post*

Susie Nickens Ludlow has written a deeply enthralling book that goes a long way in helping us understand the price African Americans have paid to get to where they are today. Readers from the Washington D.C. region, especially Virginia, the state where the Nickens family history begins and the state where the first African slaves were brought ashore, will be richly rewarded. It is a rich and vivid account of the determined family's history–from slavery to freedom. It is a must read.

Evelyn Brooks Higginbotham
Harvard University

As a child, I referred to my visits to the Nickens' home in Virginia as going to the "country."...I can still remember the idyllic serenity of this place despite the decades and places that separate me from it. The country offered something different from the ambition and pretension of my more familiar world of Washington, D.C. I did not sense its true meaning, however, until I read Susie Nickens Ludlow's fascinating and well-researched book. The green land, the house and porch, and especially the large old trees symbolized the proud and strong family roots of the Nickens clan.

This is a story of a place and its people, of a family whose ancestral mixture is Native American, African, and European. Susie Nickens Ludlow, the descendant of a long line of free blacks on her father's side and slaves on her mother's, takes her readers to the home that sheltered her and her siblings from the demeaning effects of segregation, poverty, violence and disenfranchisement... Back and forth from Washington to the Virginia farm, the book, like the Nickens family itself, weaves a personal memoir of the black middle class. Ludlow provides vivid descriptions of life and attitudes in each setting... Ultimately, this is an enduring story of family members who attained success in Washington, Chicago, Oakland, and other places, but who never failed to look homeward to the "country."

Carry Me Back

A Family and National History
of Slavery and Freedom

Susie Nickens Ludlow

Carry Me Back
Copyright © 2000 by Susie Nickens Ludlow

Front cover drawing of original
Nickens Virginia home
Copyright © 2000 by Marie Johnson Calloway

Book Design and Printing by

FALCON BOOKS

San Ramon, California

ISBN 0-9679879-0-3

Published by

Honocan Press
P.O. Box 240
5856 College Avenue
Oakland CA 94618

PRINTED IN THE UNITED STATES OF AMERICA

Dedicated to the memory of my parents,
James M. Nickens, Jr.
(1881-1952)
and Susie B. Nickens
(1885-1979)

My brother, James H. Nickens, Sr., M.D.
(1913-1996)
and sister, Elizabeth E. Nickens
(1924-1997)

Acknowledgements

I am indebted to my sister, Elizabeth Nickens, who did extensive research of wills, army pensions, land deeds and Virginia Historical Societies. She documented the Nickens family whose members were classified as free persons of color back to 1800. She also furnished the history of the black communities of that area in northern Virginia where our forbears were born and lived out their lives. I appreciate her being the keeper of the family Bibles and preserving the family pictures.

I am grateful to my nephew, James Harold Nickens, Jr., for supplying information concerning the Nickens family gathered from members of other branches of Nickens families who have researched their Nickens roots, and for his research of records in Lancaster County where our original Nickens ancestors were born.

My thanks to my family members: my brother, Harold Nickens, my sister, Eunice Le Cesne, who filled in the gaps of my memory, and my daughter, Enid Simmons, who sent me information as I requested.

My gratitude extends to Anita Halloway who deciphered the first five chapters of my handwritten manuscript and typed them into her computer; retired Col. James Stewart who corrected typographical errors on his computer; and to my D.C. friends Hestlene Martin, who mailed me materials and books I requested, and Thelma Baltimore, who furnished me with the histories of Washington social clubs.

I also would like to acknowledge Valena Williams who first planted the seed for this book when she asked me to submit a story relating to my life for a book she was compiling called *Black Women's Stories*. I submitted the chapter, "Coping with Segregation and Racism" which was written before I began this book. It was then I realized I had many stories in me I wanted to tell.

I express my sincere appreciation to my friend and neighbor, Ann Fisher, who read parts of my manuscript, praised my writing ability and encouraged me to tell my story; to my dearest friend, Marie Johnson Calloway, who drew the picture for the book cover; to my friend Estelle King who loaned me references from her library; and to Candice Trotter for her valuable contribution in critiquing one chapter.

Finally, I am forever grateful to my husband, Paul Ludlow, who patiently listened as I read segments of my manuscript; supplied a word or phrase as I sometimes groped for the right one, and freed me to spend time writing by taking over the household duties while I isolated myself in our study.

Table of Contents

Foreword

The words of my paternal grandmother, Kate Nickens, have always lingered in my memory when she admonished us, "Remember to tell your children that their grandfather's people were never slaves."

The summer my grandson, Robert Herndon, was planning to attend Northwestern University to begin work on a master's degree in film making allowed us to enjoy spending an entire day together. This gave me an opportunity to tell him about our family heritage and relate some of my life experiences.

He implored me, "Please write a book on what you have told me. My children may never get to know you. They will know you through your book and their heritage on your side of the family."

On one of my visits to our family home in Virginia I opened a trunk and found numerous notes, notebooks and documents pertaining to histories of our family and Virginia communities that had been collected by my sister, Elizabeth Nickens. I inquired as to how she intended to use this material. Her reply was that she was too involved in the community to continue her research. She asked if I would take the material, continue the research, and write it in some format.

Thus it was at the urging of my sister and my grandson that I embarked on writing this book. It is based on oral family histories, family Bible data, and Virginia Courthouse records of Fauquier, Lancaster, Louden, and Prince William Counties.

Information was also gathered from tombstones in graveyards and various history reference books.

My research consisted of information found in the genealogical section of the Library of Congress, the National Archives, the genealogy section of the Oakland Mormon Temple, Revolutionary War records and pension records.

I am impelled to write this book about my family because they strove to improve the quality of life of each generation as did so many of our people of color. We were blessed to have as parents, Susie Brown Nickens, a descendant of slave parents, and James Maxville Nickens, Jr., a descendant of free people of color whose history of freedom has been traced and documented back to Colonial America.

I have attempted to relate how the different sociological backgrounds affected each family. Much of the history of these two families has been passed down to me orally by family members: grandparents, aunts, uncles and my parents. Additional information has been documented through my research with assistance from my family members and persons from other branches of Nickens families.

This then is a narrative of my two African American families: one whose members have always been free people of color in America, the other family descended from slaves. It is an account of the perseverance of the free family to remain free through eight generations prior to the Emancipation Proclamation. They were faced with oppressive laws imposed by a system built for two societies, free whites and black slaves. My slave ancestors orally related to me the hardships they endured as slaves and their struggle to acquire property and educate their children after they were freed.

This is a chronicle of my life which spans eighty years of historical eras: segregation, Depression, three wars and integration. I relate my experience as a black woman residing in three areas of the United States: Prince William County, Virginia;

Washington, D.C.; and Oakland, California. I also weave into the story some experiences of other family members.

I expose "colorism" or light skin versus dark skin, its origins and the adverse effect that created a division in the black race.

This book's main setting is the Virginia land that the Nickens family has owned and occupied for one hundred thirty-five years. It is to this Virginia home that I have returned every year of my life to reaffirm my roots, unite with my family, recapture memories, and put my life in its proper perspective. It is through this yearly journey that I have renewed my faith in God and man.

Note: Various racial designations have been used as they related to different eras: mulatto, free persons of color, colored, Negro, black and African American. Indian and Native American are also used in this context.

Chapter One

The Beginning

No place on earth do I love more sincerely,
Than old Virginia the place where I was born.

Carry Me Back to Old Virginia
— James Bland

I have a vivid memory of my father playing the mandolin and singing the lyrics of the song by the Black composer, James Bland, *Carry Me Back to Old Virginia*. He never sang it in the original dialect in which it was written but he enunciated the words clearly. The last lines always evoked in me some indescribable emotion and feelings of nostalgia.

If I had to choose in which month to be born, it would be October. Indian Summer arrives in Virginia in mid-month, warming the earth again after a fortnight of occasional frosty nights. Soon the days begin to chill and it is then that Nature bursts forth in all her finery. The surrounding woods become an array of colors, various shades of reds, oranges, yellows and tans.

I was the third child of four children born to my parents, James Maxville Nickens, Jr. and Susie Brown Nickens. I was born October 14, 1917 in the middle of this perfect month. The period 1917-18 was one of America's most tumultuous and calamitous times. Our country was in the midst of World War I. Six months after my birth, the influenza epidemic occurred, which caused the deaths of thousands of American civilians. My parents told us that people were dying so fast the undertakers were unable to embalm and bury them all. Many Virginia families were forced to place their deceased relatives in wooden boxes and bury them in their private graveyards. My father was also a victim of this disease but fortunately he survived.

At this time, most black children in this area were born at home. When I was old enough to ask about childbirth my mother described the details of my birth. She said my birth was much more difficult than the previous births of my brother and sister. When her labor pains began, the evening prior to my delivery, my father drove one mile to bring my grandmother to stay with her. My grandmother was in attendance at the births of all her thirty-one grandchildren who were born in Virginia. Seven others were born elsewhere. My father then drove two miles to get the doctor. The only doctor available was Dr Payne, a young white doctor who had just completed his internship and was due to report to the army induction center within two days. He indicated that I was a posterior presentation and that my mother would have a long and difficult labor

In those days, the men would keep one another company during a wife's labor. My father's brother, Richard, who lived across the road, came to sit with him during the long wait. My father got his bottle of whisky, which he kept hidden in the closet under the steps. They each took one drink from a shot glass and saved the rest for another drink upon my arrival. Finally Grandma announced that Mama had a girl. As Dr. Payne was anxious to leave he then needed my name in order to fill out the birth certificate. It was customary in both families to name a child after a relative. Mama chose the name Susie so I could be named after her but Grandma insisted she wanted me to have her name, Irene. Thus I was named Susie Irene Nickens. Later when she realized my initials spelled the word SIN, Mama added Letitia, the name of a friend. Since Dr. Payne had to report for Army duty the next day, my mother received no post-natal care.

After the naming ritual, the pronouncements and predictions took place as I was inspected. This scene was repeated at the birth of every child in the family, because of the importance my family placed on retaining their mulatto characteristics. Grandma examined me and said, "Susie, she is going to have light skin like you. You, Joe and Marie were my lightest children. Look at the skin around her finger nails. It's pink, not tan; that's how you can tell what color she will be."

Mama then commented, "I don't think her hair will be as straight as Eunice and Harold. Hers feels soft; I remember the strands of their hair separated when I rubbed their hair between my finger tips."

Papa added, "Look at her legs. She is going to be short like my mother. I can tell because the length from her knees to her ankles is short."

I survived the winter and a year after my birth the soldiers began returning home. Thirty-five years after my birth, my mother and I were visiting a sick relative in the hospital when we encountered Dr. Payne. After greeting us he asked my mother, "Mrs. Nickens, I remember delivering one of your children just before I went into the army; did that child live?"

My mother replied, "Yes, this is she with me."

All four children in our family were born in the same white and brass iron bed in the second floor bedroom of the house my father built just before he married my mother. It was a framed farm house with no electricity, nor indoor plumbing. The house was located on a two hundred acre farm in Prince William County, Virginia. The farm was midway between four villages: Buckland on the west, Thoroughfare on the north, Haymarket on the east, and Gainesville on the south. Each village was within two miles of our home except Gainesville which was four miles away. My siblings and I were the fourth generation to occupy this farm and the ninth generation on my paternal side to be born free Americans.

The farm had been originally part of the Tyler Plantation. Before the trees in the woods had grown to their full height the Bull Run Mountains could be seen in the distance. It was ceded to a bachelor son, Dr. William Tyler. The Tylers were a branch of the family of President John Tyler. Woods surrounded the farm on two sides; the main section of the land consisted of fields and rolling hills. Each hill had a different color when the earth was bare, and we referred to them as the "brown hill, the yellow hill, and the red hill."

The original house owned by Dr. Tyler was located on the "red hill." It was a frame house consisting of two upstairs bedrooms, and a warming room or parlor on the first floor that was connected to a back bedroom. The kitchen was attached to the house but could not be entered from the main house. It had a separate entrance with a porch leading to the main house. Down the hill from the house ran a stream which led to a spring that supplied the drinking water. My father's brother Richard and his family occupied this house during his lifetime. We always referred to it as Uncle Dick's house. Near the house was a stable with a loft to hold hay and fodder for horse feed. Originally two hundred yards from the house existed a slave log cabin which was later torn down soon after I was born. This cabin served as a school for Negroes in 1870 when Virginia first supported public education for colored. My maternal Grandfather Brown attended this school. The Turner family were formerly the slaves who occupied this cabin and were owned by Dr. Tyler. They moved to a home in the Catharpen area.

The custom of naming a child for a relative provided some continuity in the families. Since we were told and read that the Nickens families were always free Americans we were proud that the surname Nickens was not taken from the name of a slave master.

In my family the oldest child, a son, was named James Harold. James was the first name of my father, my father's father and my mother's father. My sister was given the name Eunice Louise; her middle name, Louise, was after a maternal aunt and maternal great aunt. My mother's name, Susie, was after a maternal great aunt. My youngest sister was christened Elizabeth Estelle. Estelle was the name of my maternal grandmother's oldest sister; thus we bore the names of three generations of family members..

My family always called my brother by his middle name, Harold. I was always called Sue to distinguish me from my mother. My father was always called Mack, short for his middle name, Maxville.

Chapter Two

My Ancestors

Early in the slave trade, African-Americans valued lighter skin because it was an economic and social commodity. It could symbolize connections to European royalty or aristocracy and translate to respect. More specifically, light skin could place a slave in a favored position as the plantation master's mistress or a house slave which translated into more food, better clothing, or lighter workloads.

—Susan Marie Jenkins,
Is Light Really Right in the Lives of African-Americans?

My Maternal Roots—The Brown Family

In 1934, during my junior year at Dunbar High School in Washington, D.C., my English teacher gave us a long term assignment of writing our autobiographies. She suggested that we begin by interviewing our grandparents. Since my grandparents were living in Virginia, I decided to conduct my interviews during my spring break when my family returned to our Virginia country home for Easter vacation.

My mother had given me her parents' vital statistics, which she had secured from the family Bible. Her father, James Buchanan Brown, was born July 13, 1856 on a plantation located in Fauquier County. Her mother, Irene Snow Barbour, was born August 7, 1859 on the Lewis plantation located near a small town named Plains in Fauquier County, Virginia. They were both born slaves. Their marriage took place January 1, 1879, fourteen years after the Civil War.

I set out walking the mile from our house to Grandpa Brown's farm via Thoroughfare Road. I left in the early afternoon so I could return home before dark. I had previously written a letter to Grandpa to explain to my grandmother the purpose of my visit, as she could neither read nor write. As I turned into the lane that led to their farmhouse, I glanced at the big hickory tree where two babies were buried; one was Grandma's baby and the other one was the baby of my mother's sister, Louise.

As I approached their house, they were both standing outside the yard gate shading their eyes with their hands. "It's Little Sue," said Grandma as she was the first to recognize me.

"How you, Little Sue?" greeted Grandpa, extending a calloused hand roughened by hard labor.

Grandma and I embraced. "Come on in the house," she said. "I made a pound cake and lemonade to serve you." I remembered this was the usual repast she served her guests.

"I would like a cool drink of water from the well first," I said.

"Certainly. Rena, get me a glass from the house for Little Sue." Grandpa spoke as he drew a bucket of water.

"No, I want to drink from the dipper," I said. The gourd dipper which hung on a nail of the well post somehow made the water taste cooler and more distinctive than in a glass. I sipped the cool water and recalled the earthy flavor like spring water. We entered the kitchen and walked through to the dining room. It had been six years since I stayed with them and attended Norfolk school. My grandparents looked nearly the same as when I stayed with them. Grandpa's six-foot frame was more stooped; his wiry hair was greyer, and his red-tan complexion had few wrinkles for his age. His prominent high nose dwarfed his thin lips. Grandma's face was lined and wrinkled. She was slender and about five feet two inches in height. She combed her straight silver hair in an upsweep with a plait wound and pinned in a bun on top.

As I entered the kitchen, I saw that everything was the same as I remembered it. Three split-bottom chairs were placed at the white oil-cloth covered oak table. There was a big wood-burning, black cooking stove where Grandma cooked her delicious cornbread daily. A wooden box for firewood was beside the stove. In the corner was a built-in shelf that contained a tin bucket of drinking water and a tin dipper. Near the dining room entrance was a perforated upright tin chest where she kept dishes, pots, and pans. The floor was covered with the white and red-designed linoleum that Grandpa had bought and laid as a homecoming present for Grandma when she separated from him for several months and stayed in Philadelphia with her sister, Susie.

In the dining room was a long oak table and ten oak chairs. A mahogany rocker was beside the wood burning stove. Over the stove was a wooden mantle that held the striking clock. Grandma set it every evening by the train whistle. I often wondered whether the time was off due to the train being early or late. A wooden chaise lounge where Grandma took her daily naps was beside the wall. The dining room also contained two buffets or sideboards as they called them. One was dark oak that contained her sister Estelle's silver and dishes. The other was a tall, light oak with shelves and a mirror that contained Grandma's silver and dishes.

"Where is Aunt Estelle?" I asked.

"She is upstairs in her room. She has been ailing here of late," answered Grandma. Aunt Estelle was Grandma's oldest sister who had moved from Boston and had come to live with her after she had lost her husband and her daughter from tuberculosis. She brought her fancy furniture and dishes which she mixed with Grandma's furniture. She put her parlor furniture and

piano in Aunt Louise's house. She was a proper speaking, digni-
fied lady who always dressed up on Sundays in black outfits and
jet jewelry. She also wore gold pierced earrings and pince-nez
eye glasses.

I went upstairs to speak to her. She was a small woman,
about five feet tall, and weighed about 100 pounds. She was
happy to see me and rose from her chair to kiss and hug me. She
and Grandma had different fathers. Grandma looked to be completely Caucasian whereas Aunt Estelle was honey colored with
extremely curly, soft hair.

I returned to the dining room where Grandpa sat at his usual
place, the head of the table. A plate containing a slice of pound
cake and a glass of lemonade was set at each place. I sat next to
him facing the wall where five large, almost life-sized portraits
hung in ornate gilded frames.

As there were no tape recorders available at that time, I took a
few notes and later wrote from memory. My sister, Elizabeth, recently refreshed my memory with information she had collected. "I know who she is," I said pointing to the second picture
on the left, as I looked at my great grandmother's picture. "She is
your mother, Grandma, my Great-grandmother Hall. Tell me
about her."   •

Grandma related this information. "Her name was Emily
Jane Barbour. She was born a slave on the Barbour Plantation,
which was owned by a man who was related to Governor
Barbour and who at one time was the Governor of Virginia. She
did not know the date of her birth because the birth of slaves was
not recorded in Virginia until 1856. She thought she was born
about 1838. When Mama was quite young she had Aunt Estelle,
whose father was a slave on another plantation, owned by a
man whose name was Scott. Estelle was given the name Scott as
her maiden name.

"In her late teens, your Great-Grandma Barbour was sold to
the Lewis family who owned a plantation in Fauquier County.

She had a sister whose name I cannot recall but who later moved to Washington and married a man whose last name was Piper. She also had a brother whom Grandma called 'Uncle Sonie.' She was separated from her sister and brother when she was sold, but later was able to contact them after the Civil War." Grandma told how Uncle Sonie would come and freeload on her and Grandpa for several winters. Great-Grandma retained the last name Barbour. She worked as a house slave and had five children by Mr. Lewis, her master. All went by the surname Barbour. When my great grandmother left the Lewis Plantation, she gave birth to a boy John and a girl Miriah who were fathered by a black man. These children retained the Barbour name. She finally married a man named John Hall by whom she had two daughters, Landonia and Elizabeth.

"Did you live in a slave cabin Grandma?" I inquired.

"No, we lived with our mother in two rooms in back of the kitchen," she answered. "The kitchen was not connected to the big house. My mother's children and the Lewis children all played together until it was time to eat. The white children ate in the dining room while my sisters, brothers, and I ate from tin plates placed on the porch where we stood on the ground. In winter we ate sitting on a long bench in the kitchen."

As I gazed at the portraits, I noticed that my great-grandmother Barbour appeared to have some Indian blood but was mostly Caucasian with black, straight hair, parted in the middle and brought to the back and pinned. Next to her picture was a portrait of a pretty, blond young woman. She was my Great-Aunt Susie for whom my mother and I were named. She married a man who was mostly Caucasian and whose last name was White. They moved to Philadelphia and passed for white. She kept in touch with Grandma, who visited her once. She had two daughters who taught school in Philadelphia.

To the left of Great-grandma Barbour-Hall's picture was a portrait of a woman who looked to be full-blooded Indian except her hair had very small waves. She wore it in two thin plaits that hung to her shoulders. She was Grandpa's mother. Before her marriage to a Mr. Berry, her last name and her children's names were Brown but no one could explain why. She had five children; two girls, Annie and Lavinia, and three boys; my Grandfather, James, a son named Carroll and one named Smith. As we discussed his mother, he began to tell me of his childhood.

"My mammy's name was Mariah. She was born a slave near the Plains Virginia. When I was 'roun five years old and my sister, Annie was ten we was took from my mammy and sold to a plantation down south in Alabama. I never knew my master's name. The slaves called him Mars John. We stayed there near going on four years. Sister picked cotton and I was the water boy carrying water up and down the rows for the cotton pickers to drink. When we left the cotton fields, I had to pull weeds out of our garden that we planted in back of our cabin. Sister and I lived in a two room slave cabin with a dirt floor. We slept on wooden cots with sacks sewn together and stuffed with hay. An older woman and two other slaves occupied the cabin with us." He told how they had to work from sunup to sundown with little to eat but salt pork, hoecakes and vegetables they were able to grow in a little patch near the cabin. They also ate wild fruit and nuts: persimmons, black berries, chestnuts, black walnuts and hickory nuts. Sometimes they had possum or coon that some of the slaves caught.

"Christmas was the best time. Ole marsa let us come to the yard at the big house where folks would dance and sing for a whole week. Ole marsa giv us all new clothes then and we had good food to eat. The slaves talked about the war that was going on and that President Lincoln was going to free us. We had been there four years when the big bell rang calling us to the big house and ole marsa told us we was free. There was much shouting for joy and jubilation when we heard this news. A few stayed on the plantation where Mars John said he would pay them to work. Most started walking in search of their kin. Sister and I started walking north to find our mother who was still in Virginia. We followed the north star when we walked at night and the moss on the trees in the day that grew on the north side. Finally, we reached the Old Carolina Trail, the route the slaves were taken going south when they were sold from up north. We stopped at slave cabins along the way and some slaves would feed us and let us sleep there. At times we ate wild fruit and nuts. Sometimes people gave us rides in wagons and carts. Every so many weeks we would ask what state we were in. When someone finally said Virginia, we knew we were almost home. After we had walked for about four months, we found our mammy living at the same plantation."

I asked, "Why did you call your mother Mammy?"

"Our owners did not like us to call her Mother because that's what the white children called their mothers."

"Why did she look so much like an Indian?" I inquired.

He scratched his head and became pensive. "My mother's mother was colored and her father was an Indian. Indians used to come on the plantations and work. They had to stay with the slaves in their cabins, but they were never made slaves. After getting paid and given clothes they went back to their tribes. I reckon her father was one of those Indians."

"What did you do after you were freed?" I asked.

"We stayed on with our mother until we were old enough to be put out in service. I met your grandmother while she was working for the Carter family and I was working on a farm nearby. We got married on New Year's Day and rented a house near Gainesville, Virginia. There your Aunt Clara and your Aunt Lavinia were born. We saved enough money to put down on this farm. I went to work in the mills in Pennsylvania to help pay the mortgage off. Our other six children were born here."

"How did you learn to read, write and cipher, Grandpa?" I asked.

"I had a chance to go to school in the winter when I was fifteen and work on the farm got slack. Mos I generally learned myself." Grandpa had one brown eye and one cloudy grey eye. I knew he was blind in the grey eye.

"How did you lose your eye, Grandpa?" I asked.

"I was working on the road picking rock when a piece of rock flew into my eye and put it out. I had to work hard to make enough money to send your mother and your aunts and uncles to Manassas Industrial School. I had to pay room, board and tuition for each one. There were no public high schools in Virginia for colored at that time."

I thanked them, said my goodbyes and walked home. While walking I felt tremendous admiration for their strength and their perseverance in overcoming such daunting obstacles that enabled them to rear and educate a family of eight. I was proud to be one of the descendants of such survivors. Despite traumatic and adverse conditions, they both lived to be in their eighties with alert minds and their psyches intact to the end.

My Paternal Roots—The Nickens Family

In 1662 the Virginia legislature enacted laws prohibiting interracial marriages and declaring that children follow the status of the mother. Therefore, if a mother was free her children would be free; likewise, children born to slave mothers remained slaves for life.

Free Negro men were often denied the right to purchase large tracts of land in northern Virginia after the Revolutionary War. The white planters had their slaves learn the skilled crafts that were the former source of income of free black men. Free Negro women often did not marry, even though they headed households and had children. Their chances for marriage were lessened because slaves could not legally marry. Some slaves were allowed to perform slave marriage rituals, but their masters still had the authority to sell either one of them, often separating the "married couple". Interracial marriages were forbidden by law.

The only skilled occupations open to free women were laundering, which they charged for by the piece, and dressmaking. To avoid being forced to live in poverty, many free women of color had relationships with white men who helped to support them and any children they fathered. Often they lived as their mistresses and in turn worked as their housekeepers.

Much of the information about the Nickens family was given orally by my grandparents, my father and his siblings. Other detailed information was secured by my sister, Elizabeth Nickens, who did extensive research of birth and marriage records and listings of free Negroes in the Virginia County Courthouse. Some data was found on tombstones in the family graveyards and church records. Other statistics were listed in the family Bible and Virginia census records.

My father was the son of James Maxville Nickens, Sr. and Mary Katherine Nickens. James Maxville was born in 1852 in Warrenton, Virginia, a free man of color. He was the son of Sarah Ann Nickens, a free mulatto, who was born December 15, . 1828 in Maxville, Virginia. She was called Sally by her family. Her mother is listed as Sally Nickens, born 1799. She had one sister, Mary, born in 1834. She also had two uncles, Bernard (Barney) born in 1800 and Rubin born in 1802. All members of the Nickens family were listed in the records as free people of color.

Great-grandmother Sally became financially independent at an early age. She worked as a seamstress and was able to purchase a home in the town of Warrenton on Haiti Street where she resided and bore three sons. She and a first cousin, Elizabeth, shared the house. She also purchased two other homes in Warrenton which she rented out.

My father described her as having an olive complexion with soft, curly dark hair. Racially mixed marriages were illegal and cohabiting with slaves was frowned on by the Nickens family; therefore she had relationships with white men. Her first child, Cook, was fathered by a French cook who was employed at the Warren Green Hotel in Warrenton where Grandma Sally also worked as a seamstress for the rich guests at the hotel. My grandfather, James, was the son of a free man of color who was half Indian. Her third son, Charles Dushaun, was also fathered by the white Frenchman. Charles retained his father's surname, Dushaun. All three sons lived with her in her Warrenton House.

Grandma Sally was highly literate for a free black woman. Prior to 1831, free people of color in Virginia were allowed to receive an education. Frequently the children were sent to homes of white women who were paid by the parents to teach their offspring to read, write and cipher. In 1831 a Virginia statute prohibited free Negroes from assembling any place for the purpose of being taught to read and write. Thereafter free people of color who had been taught prior to the statute taught their own children. Virginia did not provide free public schools for Negroes until 1870. By that time my Grandfather was eighteen years old. He had, however, obtained a good basic education from his mother's teaching and by reading books available in the house that belonged to Dr. Tyler where he and his mother eventually resided. In 1861 Grandma Sally moved with her three sons to the home of Dr. Tyler, who had been ceded two hundred acres from his father's plantation known as the Tyler Plantation.

Grandma's cousin Elizabeth, who was called "Liza", moved to a house outside of Warrenton. She was the black mistress of Mayor John Marr, the mayor of Warrenton, who had this house built for her. One of her descendants said she had five children by the mayor. Liza was said to be a haughty woman. Mayor Marr had six children by his wife, and as each child was born, he had a room added to his house in Warrenton. Likewise, Liza demanded that after the birth of each of her children, the mayor add a room to her house. As a result, Liza's home was comparable in size to the mayor's house. Every Sunday after church services he would have his black coachman drive him in his glass enclosed coach out of town to Liza's. The townspeople knew the situation and accepted this arrangement. Liza also had two sons by a prosperous white man named Horner. These sons passed for white. Her sister Mary married a black man whose last name was Lucas. They lived in the Cub Run area a few miles from Warrenton. They had one son, Thomas Lucas.

Free people of color were often scorned by whites and resented by slaves. Their social life centered around family activities. They remained an insular society from colonial days up through World War II. Whenever they traveled outside their immediate community, they were required to obtain "freedom papers." This required that they bring some white person known by them to the courthouse, to swear that the individual was born free and is free. The papers gave a detailed description of their physical appearance. Grandpa said that his mother sewed the "freedom papers" in a small pouch with a flap that buttoned. She pinned them to him and his brothers whenever they left the area and warned them they might be kidnapped and sold down south as slaves if they were caught without their papers.

Tall oak and pine trees grew on a large section of Dr. Tyler's property. Agriculture devoted to the growing of corn and vegetables, livestock and lumbering constituted the main sources of income for Dr. Tyler who also practiced medicine.

The house was located five miles from Bull Run where one of the first battles of the Civil War was fought in July, 1861. Grandpa related details of the incidents he remembered that pertained to the Civil War. In the first Bull Run battle, the farmers in the area thought it would just be a skirmish. Several took their wives in buggies to watch the standoff. It turned out to be a fierce battle in which the Union troops lost. The war continued for four years from the time the family initially occupied the house. The roar of cannons could be heard for miles. Confederate soldiers were frequently seen walking or riding near the property. A second battle was fought at Bull Run in August, 1862 where the Union soldiers were again defeated. This battlefield has always been considered consecrated ground in Virginia because of these Confederate victories.

Dr. Tyler was conscripted to serve as a medical officer for the Confederate wounded. He left a loaded gun for Grandma Sally in order to protect her and her family against the intrusion of any soldiers. A hospital was set up in a stone house near the battlefield to treat Confederate soldiers. Beverly's Mill, a large, three-story stone structure, was located three miles from the Tyler house and one mile from Thoroughfare Gap, the route used by the Underground Railroad to take slaves north to freedom. This building also served as a hospital for the Confederate wounded.

During the time Great-grandma Sally lived with Dr. Tyler, she was treated as the mistress of the house. From this liaison she bore a son, William Randolph. Interestingly enough, there was a slave family who lived in a log cabin located on the property to do the farm labor. Her sons lived with her in Dr. Tyler's home until they became adults. She and all her sons retained the Nickens name with the exception of her son, Charles.

Before Dr. Tyler died, he signed a document stating that he owed Sally a large sum of money for her housekeeping services. She took this document to court and was granted a deed which enabled her to acquire the house and the two-hundred acre farm at his death. With her income saved from her seamstress work and other property holdings, she became a very prosperous woman. After the Civil War Great-grandma Sally was in a position to grant loans to the former plantation owners who had become financially destitute by financing the Confederate Army. These loans were similar to second mortgages.

For the next fifteen years after the Civil War, all southern blacks enjoyed their new freedom. The Nickens family felt free to marry within their race. The oldest son, Cook, married a mulatto and had two daughters. My grandfather, James Maxville, married Kate Chambers in 1871.

In 1870, Jim Crow laws were passed in the southern states. This began a reign of terror by the Ku-Klux-Klan. Life under these laws became so oppressive that many Negroes moved north and west to escape them. As a result, the oldest son, Cook, moved to the state of Washington with his wife and two daughters. There they passed as white. He read law and eventually practiced law. He received an appointment as minister to one of the Hawaiian Islands. He sent his daughters to Europe for their education when they were young. One daughter later became a famous singer. This was a well-kept family secret. She later made her concert debut in the United States and achieved national fame as a great singer. She eventually became a U.S. citizen where she lived the remainder of her life. She may never have known her ancestors were black .

The other two brothers, Charles and William, also settled in the Western United States. Their brother Cook kept in touch with his mother and informed her of his brothers' whereabouts and their welfare.

Grandma Sally later married a colored man, but the marriage was short lived, ending in a divorce. As she declined in years, she wanted her property and assets to go to her son, James, my grandfather. When my father was nineteen, my grandfather took him out West to look over land that might be suitable for a ranch. The trip may have reflected the family's desire to escape the Jim-Crow laws. While on the trip they contacted the other brothers who signed documents relinquishing any future claim to the Virginia property. The desolate plains of the West did not appeal to Grandpa, so they returned to Virginia to live permanently.

Grandma Sally died February 3, 1913, leaving her entire estate to my grandfather which included the two-hundred-acre
farm. This is the land that eventually has been passed to my family and other Nickens heirs. We are the fourth generation and in
some cases the fifth generation to own this land.

After my grandfather and grandmother married, he purchased a small parcel of land and a house near the Vint Hill Farm
now known as the Vint Hill Army Signal Post. Seven children
were born there including my father. The first child, Mary, died
in infancy of whooping cough. The seventh child, Randolph,
was shot and killed accidentally.

Around 1890 Grandpa Nickens moved to Washington, D.C.
to be the coachman for the president of Gallaudet College for the
Deaf. During his tenure, his family lived in a house on the campus. Three more children were born there. One of the family an-
ecdotes is the incident of Grandpa having prevented the injury
of the president of the college by stopping some runaway
horses. He was awarded a gold-inscribed watch for his bravery.

While working at Gallaudet, he purchased Ringwood, a
two-hundred-acre farm, located near Vint Hill Farm. The estate
was formerly a private finishing school for wealthy white girls.
The Nickens family used the combined school building and dormitory as their residence.

Grandpa, a shrewd businessman, contracted with the Capital Transit Company in D.C. to board the horses on his farm that
were used to pull city street cars. Three sons took six horses from
the Capital to their farm in Virginia. They alternated riding a
horse while the other horse was hitched beside them. At various
intervals, they rested. The horses were rested and fed for six
months at their farm . They then were ridden back to the Capital
and six others were taken to the Virginia farm. Grandpa retired
around 1900 and lived permanently at Ringwood as a prosperous farmer.

Grandpa farmed extensively. He constructed large, well-built farm buildings located some distance from the house: a horse barn that had eight horse stalls to hold all eight of his horses; a large cow barn and stockade for his herd of cattle; a fenced area for his hogs that contained a pig sty; and a large poultry house. As a small child, I remember the carriage house that held a surrey with a fringed top that had three double seats, and a glass enclosed coach. This building was later converted to an automobile garage.

A tenant house was located on the property a quarter mile from the main house. Grandpa allowed my father and his son Richard to live and farm on the two-hundred-acre farm he inherited from his mother. As to the mortgages held by my Great-grandma Sally, Grandpa would drive his carriage each Christmas Eve and collect payments and interest from the white farmers. When the panic of 1907 occurred, the farmers could not meet their payments. To avoid the heavy tax burden which would have been borne by Great-grandma Sally, she instructed my father to return the mortgages and cancel the balance of their loans.

When the great Depression occurred in 1929, Grandpa Nickens lost most of his liquid assets. Farming was no longer profitable. The large house was too costly to restore; the out buildings were deteriorating , farm labor was too costly and his sons had moved and obtained jobs to provide for their families. When he died in 1934 he was a man of modest means but had still maintained the four hundred acres that included both farms.

My father's mother, Mary Katherine Chambers, was born in 1854 and listed as a free black. Her father was a white man of Scottish and Irish descent whose last name was Brawner. Her mother, Emily Chambers, was also born free. She was employed as a seamstress who occupied the servants' quarters of the plantation owners' homes where she would remain for several months at a time sewing for the family. She was an expert seamstress, often copying French designer dresses for the mistress of the house. During her employment on these plantations, she gave birth to four children who all carried her surname, Chambers. Their names were Richard, Lucian, Victoria and my grandmother Kate.

We always referred to our grandmother as Grandma Kate. She retained much of her Irish culture. Born on St. Patrick's Day, she used to entertain us by dancing the Irish Jig at her birthday parties while her sons played the fiddle. She boiled most of the food she prepared and was famous for her kidney stews. To relax, she would smoke a corn cob pipe, a habit that began when she was thirty years old and continued until her death.

The following story was related by my father and his mother concerning Grandma Kate's younger brother, Lucian Chambers. During the Civil War when Lucian was seven years old, the Union Army occupied the area where Lucian's mother worked. He would often go and talk to the Union soldiers who befriended him. One Union Army Captain showed a particular fondness for him. When the Captain returned to his family in Boston, he took Lucian with him. Since Lucian looked nearly white he reared him along with his children. The family never knew what had become of him. His disappearance remained a mystery for over thirty years, until one day a man from the area where my grandparents lived went to work in Boston. While eating in a restaurant he sat near this handsome colored man and they struck up a conversation. During the conversation, the man learned his name was Lucian Chambers. They also discovered they both were originally from Virginia. The man concluded that this must be the long lost relative of Kate Chambers Nickens. Lucian immediately wrote to Grandma Nickens informing her of his whereabouts and that he would be coming home soon to see her. My father remembers my grandmother shouting with glee and rejoicing when she received the news.

When Uncle Lucian arrived at his sister's, there was even more rejoicing and tears of joy. The family threw a big party to celebrate his return. He related the story of his disappearance. He had married a woman from New Orleans and become a seaman working as a steward on commercial ships. Subsequently, Lucian frequently visited his sister at the end of his sea voyages.

Grandma Kate always impressed upon her grandchildren that our people were never slaves. "Do you mean your parents and Grandpa's parents were free?" I inquired.

Her answer was adamant: "The Nickens family were born in this country many generations ago as free people of color and were never held in slavery. As far back that anyone can remember my people were also free. My mother avoided telling us details about her parents' people. I have often wondered if her reluctance was due to the shame she felt that her grandmothers never married their children's father."

On the other hand, the Nickens family was proud of their long history of freedom. They were not ashamed of their white blood nor of the illegitimacy that resulted from unions between the Nickens and Chambers women and white men. They emphasized that these were romantic relationships between the women and their white lovers who provided protection and security for them.

The Nickens and Chambers families had a long history of literacy. My family has copies of letters Grandma Sally wrote on behalf of her relatives.

Chapter Three

Our Virginia Home

How dear to my heart are the scenes of my childhood,
The old oaken bucket that hung in the well.

From the song, *Old Oaken Bucket*
— Samuel Woodworth

"Don't step on it! don't step on it!" I kept crying and telling my sister and brother. My father had put down a new linoleum rug in the kitchen. It was bordered with flowers. The wood floor edged it, and I wanted everyone to walk around the rug on the floor. This is my earliest memory of any incident; I was thee years old at the time.

As a child, I was always so proud of any new furnishings that came into the house. I remember the beautiful grey and white speckled enameled stove that replaced the old black cook stove. It heated the water in the tank that was attached. The two top warmers had wheat designs on a white background as did the oven. We could sit by this stove and feel the warmth without getting burned.

The house was a yellow frame with dark green shutters and a tin roof. An "A" was in the middle of the roof. It faced the Thoroughfare road where our mailbox was located. Later, Mr. Harrison, a very rich farmer, built a toll road that ran in the back of the house. All residents who lived on the road paid a ten cent toll.

Other travelers paid twenty-five cents. After the road was built
my father made the back the front to face the new road. He built
a front porch with large round pillars. He also added a new
kitchen with a basement. One entered the basement through a
trap door in the kitchen where steps led to the basement. The
old kitchen became the living room.

Surrounding the house were several towering oak trees, two
walnut and one hickory tree. This made the yard at least ten degrees cooler than most spots. In the front yard was a well with
two oaken buckets attached to a chain on a pulley. When one
was pulled down the other would rise filled with cold water.
The well never went dry even in the 1927 drought. When other
neighbors' wells became dry we allowed them to fill containers
with our water for their drinking water. A low cement platform
was built around the well. This was a gathering place for the
men who visited Papa and for the farm workers to rest during
their breaks. Often a glass jar containing corn whiskey would be
shared; however, I never saw my father intoxicated.

A wooden plank fence surrounded the yard. Eunice and
Harold had the task of whitewashing it each spring, one on the
outside and the other on the inside. This led frequently to whitewashing duels when one pretended to inadvertently stick the
brush through and paint the other.

The house had the usual out buildings: a barn, hen house,
smoke house to cure meats, a garage and a toilet. In the back was
a grape arbor and an orchard that burst forth with blossoms each
spring. A vegetable garden was beyond the orchard. There were
only two houses in view, Uncle Dick's and the Berry house located several fields away on a hill. The Berrys were my mother's
first cousins. Other prosperous farms owned by whites bordered our farm.

I learned to distinguish between east and west at an early
age. As we watched the big orange ball in the sky drop out of
view behind the tall trees in the woods, Papa sometimes sang a

few lines of "Day is Dying in the West." Other times in the day a long dark ominous cloud formed and hung over the same spot. When that happened Papa would say, "We are going to have a big thunderstorm. That cloud is hanging over Hannah's Hole." His prediction always proved true.

I was always afraid in thunderstorms. Our parents called us into the house and shut all windows and doors. At various times lightning struck trees near our house. Mr. Lake's barn was struck by lightning and burned to the ground. His farm adjoined our farm.

On clear nights we could see a faint glimmer of lights in the opposite direction.

"What are these lights in the sky, Mama?"

"That is the City of Washington. It is in the East and is forty miles from here."

The quietness of the place has always remained in my memory. Now and then a farm animal broke the stillness. One could hear a car approaching a quarter of a mile down the road before it came in sight. If we were in the yard playing, the first one who heard a car would yell, "My car!" That one had to claim that car no matter how it looked. Often it was a rattle trap; sometimes it was a big luxury car.

Each sound of nature had some meaning for us. The honking of the wild geese ushered in spring. The katydid's humming meant it would be hot the next day. The whippoorwill's call meant it was time to stop playing and come and sit on the porch. It was then my father would play the mandolin and sing songs for us. Soon it was time to wash our feet and undress for bed.

When the song "My Blue Heaven" became popular we would sing,

"When Whippoorwills call, and evening is nigh, I'll hurry to my blue heaven."

Chapter Four

Childhood Years

Though time may pass, a memory stays,
Reminding us of happy days,
And of the people who have touched our lives.
A memory is a treasure that survives.

—Amanda Bradley

The colored schools closed the last day in April which meant an eight month school term. The white schools continued until June first.

Each year when the first of May arrived, Mama would let us take off our shoes and go barefoot. The first few days our feet were so tender that even the grass tickled the bottoms. Within a few days our feet toughened and we went barefoot for the rest of the summer. We only wore our patent leather slippers and Harold wore his oxfords when we went to church or to some social gathering.

When I reminisce, those summer days were the happiest times of my youth. Papa put up a swing with a flat board for the seat, strung with wire and looped over a limb. He made a spring board for us to play on. We would climb to the top and it would bounce us over the fence. We played "Highover", a game where you threw the ball over the house to the person on the other side. If the person caught it he would sneak around the house and hit the other with it. We played "Hide Go Seek" and "Polly Wants a Corner".

There was a sand pile in the yard where we built houses. Harold could build castles that were superior to our houses. "Show us how to build one," we would beg. "No, then yours would be as good as mine and I want Papa to see mine," was his usual response.

We enjoyed summer social events; a field day was held in a field on our farm where community teams played baseball and sometimes games on horses similar to a joust, throwing a long stick through a large hoop attached to a tree limb as they raced. Mama and Aunt Susie Dick set up tables and sold food. Three brothers had each married women named Susie; therefore, my aunts were called Aunt Susie Cook and Aunt Susie Dick, and Mama was Aunt Susie Mack. Attendees in automobiles were charged twenty-five cents admission. One summer a tall young adult attended one of the events and walked around strumming a ukulele. He was related to several of my cousins from different families. "That's Charles Drew," someone remarked. "He goes to college at Amherst." He later became famous as the doctor who invented the "blood bank", a method of preserving blood plasma. There were picnics in the grove on Madison Butler's place that had a band stand where musicians from Washington performed. One year a cousin held me up to see the pianist. "That's Duke Ellington," she said. This was before he became na-tionally famous.

The best time was when we attended the Manassas Horse Show. It was held for two days the Sunday preceding Labor Day and on Labor Day. The show was owned by a cooperation which included three of my uncles and other black business men. The horses that participated were loaned by owners of horse farms. People came from far and near in cars and on trains. The trains stopped at the show grounds to allow the passengers to disembark. In addition to watching the horses perform, there was a carousel which we rode as long as our money held out. There was also a dance pavilion where the young adults danced. A jazz band from Washington provided the music. Some years the dancers performed new dances, "the Charleston," "the black bottom," "Balling the Jack," in addition to the one steps and two steps. Some of the tunes still resonate in my mind: "Yes, We Have No Bananas," "Bye, Bye Black Bird," and "Am I Blue?"

Eunice and I had our cousins Katie and Helen, Uncle Dick's two youngest daughters, for playmates. Katie was three years older than Eunice. Helen was a year younger than I. Nevertheless, age differences did not affect our compatibility. We visited each other's home frequently. Harold had no male playmate. Occasionally a neighbor boy or cousin came to play with him; otherwise Papa was his companion. My baby sister being born into the family late had no playmates.

Harold began working for farmers from age ten, thinning corn. He was taught to save half the money he made; the other he was allowed to keep for himself and spend it the way he wished. He usually bought books as there was no public library.

The mailbox was located about one hundred fifty yards from the house on Thoroughfare Road in back of our house which was reached by a path. There was only one box with the name Nickens Brothers printed on it to serve both families. The prior day's paper, the *Times Herald,* arrived by mail. It was our duty to get the mail. Mr. Sweeny our mailman drove a horse drawn coach containing the mail. Our house was one of the last stops. By the time he arrived his face was as red as a beet and he appeared to almost fall out of the coach when he leaned over to hand us our mail, due to nipping his bottle of spirits along the way. The horse knew instinctively to stop.

Papa read the headlines to us when we handed him the paper. I remember large lettered head lines that read "PRESIDENT HARDING DIES". The paper said he died from food poisoning.

Rumors spread that he committed suicide as a result of a scandal. Others said his wife poisoned him because he had a mistress.

We read the funnies that contained "Toots and Casper", "Mutt and Jeff", "Tillie The Toiler" and several other comic strips. Papa worked the crossword puzzle.

Since the stores did not have adequate refrigeration we rarely had beef. Occasionally Papa brought a piece of beef from Washington. One time a cow we had named "Pidy" fell in a ditch and broke her leg. Papa shot her and he and Uncle Dick butchered her. They divided the beef and we had a supply of beef for a while. I could not eat it because I was reminded we were eating old "Pidy". It was a long time afterward before I began to eat beef.

Papa read to us on cold winter days, *Five Little Peppers*, *Uncle Remus Tales* and Longfellow poems including *Hiawatha*.

He enjoyed playing practical jokes on us. One summer he put up a large tent for our playhouse. Eunice and I worked all day dividing it into rooms and furnishing it with our doll furniture. We planted a package of flower seeds in the ground. The next day we went to the window to see the tent and there were blooming flowers around it. I was young and gullible enough to say, "Look, Eunice, our flowers grew over night." Eunice, seeing Papa laughing, said, "Papa picked some flowers and put them there."

We hated to see the first goldenrod appear which meant summer was almost over and time to go back to school. Late October the wild geese flew in a "V" formation going south honking the end of fall. Papa made a Jack-O-Lantern for Halloween. We did not know about "trick or treat"; besides, there were no houses nearby. We celebrated Thanksgiving with the traditional feast.

Christmas was the magic time. The house was filled for a week with the aroma of pies, cakes, and cookies baking. On

Christmas Eve we went out in the field and selected a Christmas tree which Papa would cut and we helped carry it to the house to stand in a corner for Santa Claus to trim. That night, after a supper of oyster stew we sang carols until bedtime. On Christmas morning after waking our parents a dozen times during the night to ask, "Is it time?" we went down stairs according to age, the youngest going first. Besides the excitement of seeing our new toys that Santa had brought, we would burst our hog bladders that had been blown up and allowed to dry and expand since the hogs were killed. Papa blew them up by inserting a turkey quill in the opening. We jumped on them to burst them. This was originally a slave custom that was passed down from my Mother's side of the family. We would then go to see our cousins Katie's and Helen's toys. Later Mama loaded food in Harold's wagon which we took to two different invalids' homes who lived nearby. We returned home for a Christmas feast.

At Easter we dyed eggs for Mama and Papa to hide and we hunted for them. We continued this tradition with all family members returning to our Virginia home for an Easter egg hunt for three generations. Celebrating Independence Day on July fourth was another tradition our family continued for three generations. We all gathered at the Virginia home place each year to eat and shoot fireworks at night in the very field we used when we were children.

Fall brought hunting season and hog killing time. Papa and Uncle Dick farmed as a team. We had a work horse named "Tootsie" and Uncle Dick had one named "Topsy". They worked as a pair when they farmed. We also had a riding horse on which Eunice and Harold rode to school together. Papa had a coon hunting dog named "Mose" and Uncle Dick had one named "Queen". They hunted them together. An argument would ensue after a night's hunting as to whose dog treed the coon first.

Mama returned to teaching school when I was two years old. She had a Mrs. Sea keep Eunice and me the first year. The next year she took Eunice to school with her and started her in first grade when she was five. Harold walked to North Fork School in Thoroughfare with our older cousins. I was left with Grandma and Grandpa Brown during the school week. Although I would bring my dolls with me I was very lonely and began sucking my thumb. This habit continued until I was eight years old. It caused me to develop malocclusion. Grandma was very caring and pampered me. Grandpa was somewhat of a stern person, but was always kind to me. When he went to the store he always brought me a bag of peppermint sticks and hohound candy. Grandma always looked the same for the twenty-seven years I knew her. Next to Mama my relationship with her was the closest of any woman.

Their place was a mile from our house. Eunice and Harold walked with me on Sundays to stay with my Grandparents during the week. To keep me from crying when they left they would pretend to play "Hide Go Seek" and make me "it". When I went to look for them they would have left for home.

My grandparents' house was a large farmhouse, containing a kitchen, two parlors and a large dining room that served as a dining and sitting room. There were five bedrooms. Hanging on the dining room wall were several almost life sized portraits of her and Grandpa's dead relatives. I was afraid to go in that room alone because wherever I went their eyes would stare and follow me.

There were other fears that developed while I lived with her. Whenever I was naughty she never physically abused me, but would say, "The Boogy man will get you." I conjured up an image of the "Boogy man" as a dark figure with horns and boogers running out of his nose. That deterred me from straying too far from her. When a black cloud gathered in the sky Grandpa would say, "There's a big storm abrewing. I must put the horses in the barn." Afterwards he would come in the house, go to his room and read the Bible. Grandma would take me in the dining room with her, pull down the dark green shades which darkened the room and lie on the chaise lounge with her hands folded and her eyes closed. I was warned not to make a sound. When a loud clap of thunder was heard she would say, "God is angry with somebody."

She and Grandpa occupied separate bedrooms. I slept in the bed with her. Each winter night she heated a brick, wrapped it in a towel and placed it at my feet. Sometimes she put a large glass bottle with hot water at my feet.

I was fascinated as I watched her dress in the mornings. She sponged off in the wash bowl on the wash stand, then began putting on her layers of petticoats under her gingham skirt. She let her hair down which fell to her waist, bent over, plaited it in one big braid then wound and pinned it on top of her head. The stray silky strands were held in place by two side combs.

A feisty, energetic little woman, she would often defy Grandpa when they argued. He would threaten her with an object and she would shake her fist in his face and say, "I dare you." I never saw him actually physically abuse her. Unable to read and write, she could count and figure as fast as anyone. When she sold her produce which she weighed on her scales, she calculated the exact amount that was owed. She often walked from her house to our house, carrying a stick to kill a snake if she saw one, reached in her apron pocket, pulled out a cookie, then turned around without resting and said, "I just came to bring a sweet for little Sue." She continued to do this for her great grand child.

No one had to explain to me about the birds and the bees; I received my sex education through the natural functions of living things on the farm. One morning Papa announced, "I'm taking Dolly (our cow) to be with Davis' bull."

I cried, "Oh don't take her to Davis' bull; he will kill her."

We were always warned never to walk inside the fence of the Davis field because there was danger the bull might kill us.

Papa explained, "He will just rub against her to make her have a calf. That makes her give milk."

That explanation satisfied me. I learned when the rooster jumped on top of the hen it was to make her lay the eggs that hatched into chickens. I observed the dogs mating and concluded that made the female have puppies. My brother and sister had learned about the mating of humans from our older cousins. It was explained to them in the most basic terms which they explained to me. Harold used the childish names Mama had taught us to use for genitalia. "The man puts his 'thing' in the woman's 'pee pee' and that's called doing it," Harold told me.

Once when I was playing "I Spy", an older male distant cousin who came to the house to work for Papa was sitting on a tree stump behind the house. When I went near him to hide he asked me to come and sit on his lap. I was going on five years old and many male relatives were affectionate with me; I thought he was going to give me a hug. Instead when I looked down, his pants were open and he was exposing his "thing". He took my hand and put it on it. I had never seen a man's penile erection; my father was always careful not to expose himself. I had seen my brother's as a boy and watched little boy babies being diapered, but this frightened me so I jumped off his lap and ran in the house and washed my hands. The incident had a profound effect on me and my attitude regarding sex. It didn't dawn on me that I would grow to accommodate the man; I was always afraid that sex would be impossible for me. As a result, I think I was one of the oldest virgins in college. The worst part about the incident was that I was unable to tell anyone.

My mother later tried to explain where babies came from in a most indirect way. She was cooking pancakes and never looked at us when she told us Aunt Louise had to go to the hospital because the doctor had to cut the baby out of her stomach.

"How did the baby get in her stomach?" I asked.

She said, "The father planted his seed in the mother and it grew inside the mother until it became a baby."

When we left the kitchen my brother said, "Don't you know how the baby gets into the mother's stomach? It gets there by the parents doing it."

I was abashed at this explanation and thought about it all day. Later I told them, "This can't be true because Joseph didn't 'do it' to Mary and she had Jesus."

Eunice explained, "His birth was different because God put him in Mary's stomach." This knowledge made me very sad, thinking I could not have a baby. While attending the McRae School in the Settlement, I was even more confused when I observed that women had children without husbands.

One summer my father attended summer sessions offered teachers at Manassas Industrial School. He was able to get a teacher's certificate and began as the other teacher in the two room McRae School where my mother taught. Mama taught grades one through three and Papa taught grades four through seven. I was six years old the year he began teaching so they took me to school with them, at times riding in a car or buggy depending on the weather. Eunice went to the North Fork School in Thoroughfare with Harold where Aunt Louise taught. The McRae school was located in what we called the "Settlement."

Just after Thanksgiving that year Mama stopped teaching and another teacher substituted for her. New Years morning not only ushered in 1924, but my baby sister Elizabeth was born. She looked like a little Indian papoose. Mama extended her maternity leave for two months and taught me while she kept me home with her. In March she resumed teaching, employing my great Aunt Estelle to care for Elizabeth. She nursed Elizabeth when she returned home.

There was always mutual respect between Papa and white farmers and merchants in the communities. He resented the absurdity of poor white people who felt because of their race they were superior to him.

Whenever we stopped at Buckland store old Tom Delaplane would be sitting on a wooden keg on the porch. He was a dimwitted white man with one eye, who lived with his spinster sister in Buckland. He would come to the store everyday and sit around. Every one was aware he was a kleptomaniac and when he would leave the store the storekeeper would tell him to put the article back that he had stolen. Tom would reach in his pocket and put it on the counter. One day he was in the store with his sister. When she was leaving she missed her gloves. Those in the store helped her look for them when Tom pulled them out of his pocket and said, "I didn't know they were yours." He would ask papa whenever he saw him, "Mack, how much do they pay you for teaching school?" Papa would answer, "They give me some old clothes every now and then." When the convicts were working on the road everyday he would ask them, "What are you in for?" Most would refuse to answer. One told him once, "I killed a man for asking too many questions." Tom stopped asking after that.

Once Papa hired two poor white men to work for him trimming trees. To show their "superiority" they called each other Mr. Lanham and Mr. Payne, then deliberately called him "Mack". Papa was paying them and giving them orders. He didn't say anything about the ridiculous situation. Instead, he came in the house laughing and deriding them for their show of superiority. Another time he told us about going to this white man's house on business. A woman answered his knock and told him to go to the back door.

"What happened to your wife?" Papa asked.

The man replied, "Oh that woman was too dirty. She kept dishes piled up in the sink all the time. I couldn't even take a leak in it." Yet Papa could not enter the front door.

Some poor white children came through our property to catch the school bus. Sometimes they asked to come in the house to keep warm. Often one would stare at the table where we had eaten breakfast and say, "I'm hungry." Mama usually gave them a biscuit or whatever was left over.

Papa expressed his disgust at that situation when they left, saying, "These children can come through my property to wait at my gate and be taken to school in a warm bus; whereas my children have to walk two miles to school."

He never expressed hatred toward them, only at how unfairly the system treated his children.

Those were the good years for us. No one locked their doors at night or day. There was no crime except in the Settlement area when occasionally some Saturday night drunks might get into fights with each other. The air was pure because the residents walked, rode horses, or drove horse and buggies. Very few people owned cars in the area during the 1920s.

If we were considered poor by the standards of rich whites we never felt we were. Papa always owned a car. The farm provided sufficient food. Mama sewed continually making pretty outfits for us. The old residents were cared for by one of the grown children and died at home surrounded by family. All members of both of my families lived to a ripe old age; therefore we were spared sorrow. We had no roller skates or bicycles, no radios, no Saturday matinee movies, but we had streams where we fished, a field to play baseball, outdoor play equipment which Papa built and Uncle Dick's hill to slide down on our handmade sleds when the snow was deep. We had haystacks to slide down and a ride on Tootsie when we met Papa at the road gate.

Chapter Five

My Family and Extended Family

The family is not only the basic fabric of human existence, it is the one thing that truly makes life worth living.

"Family" from *Reflections on Life and Love*
—James M. Richardson, M.D.

With the exception of my father, all his siblings married men and women from families that had been free for several generations. Those families were referred to as "old issue"; those recently freed were called "new issue". Mama was a descendant from parents who were "new issue". Both families were mulattoes and property owners. The Nickens family had owned land longer and had larger land holdings.

Other similarities in their cultural patterns existed. They maintained standards of conduct to perpetuate traditions of family life that set them apart from the Negro masses. They both formed a narrow circle of their own families and created their own society to insure an environment conducive for rearing their children to continue their way of life. Members of both families spoke standard English and avoided speaking in a black dialect with the exception of Grandpa Brown who occasionally lapsed into speaking in a slave dialect. Mama's family were strict grammarians with a pedantic enunciation. All members of both families were literate except my maternal grandmother; the

Nickens family had a longer history of literacy. There were some differences in child rearing and life styles that I attributed to the generations of freedom the Nickens family enjoyed as opposed to the Brown descendants, being born of parents who were originally slaves.

My father met my mother when she taught school near his family's home in Greenville. He courted her for three years before she consented to marry him.

In recalling my parents' physical characteristics and personalities from my memory as a child, my mother was a tall woman, five feet eight inches, light complexioned with long semi-straight hair. She wore it in a bun in the back or on top of her head. At times she wore braids wrapped around her head and pinned. I received much pleasure combing and brushing her hair which fell over the chair back to her waist. She had narrow hips, a small waist and large pendulous breasts.

She was quiet and introspective, often appearing to be day dreaming. She said to me once, "Sue, I notice you day dream a lot; what do you day dream about?" I said, "That I marry and have lots of children and live in a beautiful home." She said, "I dream of having a beautiful home one day, but I also dream that you children will finish college and become successful professionals."

She rarely laughed and lacked a sense of humor. Although she was a caring and devoted mother who lived and sacrificed for her children, she rarely displayed affection with us. A strict disciplinarian, she often switched our legs after making us get our own switches. If we brought one back that was small with leaves on the end she would make us bring another larger one with no leaves. The switches came off an orange blossom bush in the corner of the yard.

Our children tell us she administered the same type of punishment when she kept them, using switches from the same bush. We still laugh when we recall an incident when she was whipping my brother Harold, and kept asking with every whack, "Are you going to do it anymore?" My brother finally cried, "You are whipping me so I can't talk." All he had to say was, "No Mama," but that was his way of rebelling against her method of discipline.

She never learned to play cards nor dance. Her one hobby was fishing. I never knew if this was for pleasure or to put more food on the table. The only time she sang was when she was sewing on the sewing machine. She worked constantly doing household chores, washing in a tin tub using a wash board and octagon soap. She ironed with flat irons which she heated on the cook stove. She also kept busy gardening and raising chickens and turkeys.

I often wondered if she were unhappy living the hard life of a farmer's wife, though she was always loyal and caring for my father. She had a gold bracelet that expanded when you put it on your wrist. It had a place for two pictures when you opened the locket. She told us a suitor she had when she was staying in Washington gave it to her. He later became a principal of a Junior High School in D.C. When we asked, "Why didn't you marry him?" She replied, "I wouldn't have you beautiful looking children if I had," implying that he was too dark.

When she was in her early eighties and living with my sister Elizabeth in D.C. after my father passed, she was interviewed by a reporter from the *Washington Post* newspaper. This reporter was writing an article on old romances of women at different age groups. Mama was the oldest; others were in their seventies, sixties, fifties, and forties. Mama told of a teacher she had when she was in high school named Steve Lewis. She told the story beautifully, of how they often held hands and took walks together. He left to go to Dental School and later became a dentist. They exchanged gifts; he gave her a book of poems and she gave him a man's shirt collar. In those days men wore detachable collars made of celluloid and covered in white cloth. They could change their collars without changing their shirts. Mama's ending sentence was, "But we never kissed." My brother refused to read the article since it was not about our father.

Teaching school was what she liked best to do. She was an excellent teacher and her spirits would soar when the school year began each year. By teaching she was able to use her knowledge and creative ability in the classroom.

My father was the antithesis of my mother's personality. He was the same height as my mother, short by male standards. At the time of my birth he was thirty-four and completely bald on top. The rim of hair left was straight. For some years he let one side grow long which he brushed across his top. When the wind blew that hair stood up. He eventually cut it off. His skin color was a reddish tan, the color of Indians. He was always obese, weighing about two hundred pounds. A jolly, playful and sociable person, he loved to visit and converse with people. He was a warm and affectionate father who often kissed us and held us on his lap. My mother rarely if ever kissed us when we were small.

My father played games with us and sang and read to us. I remember when we dressed in our best clothes he would sing,

"Who's that girl all dressed in blue?
A pretty little girl whose name is Sue."
Or
"Who's that girl all dressed in green?
The prettiest little girl I've ever seen."

Occasionally Papa whipped my brother with a switch when he caught him in a lie. He never whipped us girls as opposed to my mother's corporal punishment. He was the dominant force in our family and today would be termed "chauvinistic" as he never helped with housework. He often displayed impatience and seemed to expect my mother to be a miracle worker. When we went on an outing, Mama would have to fix the food, dress herself and supervise the dressing of all four children. Papa would dress himself and go sit in the car, often blowing the horn for us to hurry.

In my family we were made keenly aware of our color and hair. Mama saw to it that we only associated with children that were our own color and ilk. My brother, Harold, had the darkest skin, the color of East Indians. He had straight black hair and keen features. My mother tells of the time Papa took him to visit his parents when he was about four years old. When he returned home he told Mama, "Grandma said I am the blackest thing in the family." This remark had a strong impact on his self-esteem. From the time he was a child, throughout his life, he resented being classified as a black person. My sister Eunice had olive skin and long straight black hair which my mother curled on special occasions. My younger sister Elizabeth was the same physical type and strongly resembled Eunice. I had the lightest skin in the family but had the curliest hair that did not grow beyond my shoulders. I, too, was made to feel different at various times by some of my relatives. They would make an insensitive remark such as, "Susie, whom do you think she took after?" or "You certainly have two beautiful daughters." Mama would reply, "Sue has the best personality."

I have warm memories of our family visiting my Nickens grandparents at their Ringwood farm. Harold was spared his usual chore of opening and closing gates when we entered other farm properties. The entrance gates at Ringwood were swung open and closed by the driver pulling poles attached to the gates. The house was situated a quarter mile from the road. As we rode to the house we observed Grandpa's livestock grazing in fenced fields. We never informed them of our plans to visit but were always warmly welcomed and fed. Colored people were denied the ownership of telephones in the rural areas of Virginia at that time due to the existing party-line system. The white people did not want colored people listening to their conversations.

My early recollection of the physical characteristics of my grandfather was that he was medium height and heavily built. My father was not only named for him but resembled him more closely than any of his brothers: same coloring and bald head rimmed with mixed grey hair of similar texture.

Grandma Nickens was honey colored and fine featured with straight, greying hair piled in a bun on top of her head. She was four feet, ten inches tall and never weighed over ninety-eight pounds.

In cool weather we were entertained in the large kitchen warmed by the big cooking stove. Grandma and Grandpa always sat side by side in straight chairs near enough for them to occasionally touch each other while conversing. We occupied the long benches placed on each side of the long kitchen table. In warm weather they sat on the back porch off the kitchen and entertained us.

I have a child's vision of Grandma dressed in a grey cotton handmade dress pinned at the high neck with a jeweled pin; her skirt was covered with a black and white-checked gingham apron with a large pocket where she kept her can of Prince Albert tobacco to fill her corn cob pipe. She puffed on her pipe all during our conversations. At some time during our visits, Grandpa swooped up a young grandchild toddler whom he held in his lap while Katie, their daughter, was bustling in the room preparing food.

It was during these visits and family discussions that I learned of my Nickens ancestors and their long line of freedom. Their youngest daughter, Katie, lived with her parents during their lifetime. Two other sons, Macon and Fred, lived with their families nearby on the Ringwood property.

I especially remember one of my family's visits to Ringwood when I was eight years old. On this particular visit I learned of my native American heritage.

It was in early spring and there was a chill in the air. My grandparents and my parents sat around the big cook stove in the large kitchen while Aunt Katie cooked dinner. We four children sat on one of the long benches at the table. Grandma puffed on her corn cob pipe. Grandpa held one of Aunt Katie's children in his lap. They were recollecting names of some of their kin folks when Papa asked Grandpa, "Papa, who was your father?" Papa continued, "I recall when we were small and lived on the other farm. Some men walked up to the yard. As they approached Mother hurried us into the house.(The Nickens children called their mothers "mother" as opposed to Grandpa Brown who referred to his mother as "Mammy.") We asked who they were and her answer was 'Some dirty old Indians. I don't want you near them because they have diseases.' You, Papa, went to the fence to talk with them, then gave them a sack which they filled with fruits and vegetables that they had picked from the orchard and the garden. When they left, you told us they were some cousins asking for food. How were they your cousins?"

Grandpa drew on his pipe as he reflected, "I really never got to know my father. When I asked my mother why was I a different color from my brothers she explained that my father was the son of a free colored woman and a Pamunkey Indian. Indians used to be paid to work on nearby plantations. Occasionally they came to Warrenton to purchase things. Some were taught to read and write. My mother had a relationship with this half-Indian. She pointed him out to me once. He later left and joined his father's tribe."

Aunt Katie joined in the conversation. "Mother, do you remember when we attended Double Poplar Church, a man came and sat in the back. You turned around and whispered to me, 'that's your father's father.' He was brown skinned and wore his hair long and tied back. He left the church early, mounted his horse and rode away. He didn't speak to us."

My brother Harold spoke up. "I have a shoe box containing arrowheads. Papa and Uncle Dick occasionally found them when they plowed the fields and gave them to me."

Grandpa explained, "Much of that land was woods. Indians were allowed to hunt deer and wild animals but they were forbidden to kill farm animals."

Aunt Katie told us dinner was on the table and invited us to eat. After dinner Mama helped her clear the table and do the dishes. Grandpa brought out Papa's old banjo which he had left there when he learned to play the mandolin.

"Play a song for us, Mack," Grandpa said. Papa played and sang "Fly Round Old Joe Clark". Grandma requested "Just Before the Battle, Mother" which he played and sang. Some form of music was always performed or we listened to gram-o-phone records whenever we visited a Nickens family. They never played "gut bucket blues" which was referred to as black folks' music; instead, they sang or played "Hill Billy" country and folk songs. Yodeling Billy Rogers was their favorite singer on records. Their speech patterns and accent were similar to the rural white people of the area. This leads me to believe they absorbed the culture of the rural white people and had little socialization with the rural black culture of that era. By contrast I never heard any form of music in my mother's parents home; not even hymns were sung.

I remember our trips to Manassas, located ten miles from our home. On our way Papa usually stopped at the grocery store and bought cheese and crackers for us to eat. Mama brought a jar of water or sometimes lemonade which we drank in our folding tin cups. Upon reflection I realize this was to prevent us from asking to eat in the segregated eating establishments in town.

Our trips to Manassas had a threefold purpose—a visit to the only colored doctor in the county or for dental care by the white dentist, to purchase clothes, and to visit my mother's sister Marie and her brother Joe.

Marie had married a prosperous businessman who owned a blacksmith shop which later became an auto repair shop after cars became the main mode of transportation. They had nine children and lived in a large house in the center of town. We enjoyed the luxury of using her indoor toilet with running water in lieu of the outdoor toilet to which we were accustomed. Roscoe owned seven other houses in the area which he rented. Above his shop was a movie theater that he allowed us to attend free. They were silent movies and his grown daughter played the piano to accompany the movement of the figures on the screen.

We also visited Mama's brother Joe who owned a blacksmith/auto repair shop in Manassas. He had received his training as a blacksmith at Manassas Industrial School. He lived with his family in a large house surrounded by several rental dwellings which he owned.

Our most exciting family visits were our trips to Washington, D.C. to visit Papa's sister Geneva and her family, and his brother Cook and family. They lived in the Brightwood area which at that time was practically rural. The houses in the colored area did not have indoor plumbing nor electricity. They lived in large homes to accommodate their large families; nevertheless, they always had room for our family to spend the nights.

Papa took us to the zoo where we could eat our hot dogs and drink our sodas inside the diners because they were located on federal property.

We had to drive through the city to reach their residential area. I was in awe of the city sights and sounds: the clanging of the street cars, "a-oo-ga" sound of the horns on the model T fords, and the beeping of horns on the larger cars; the clip-clop of horses hooves on paved streets and colored vendors hawking their wares.

"Fresh fish, fresh fish."

The plaintive chant of the watermelon man,

"Ice cold water melon, red to the rind,

Twenty-five cents a piece
And we plug 'em every time."
We visited my mother's youngest brother, Franklin, who
lived in town. He had been trained in carpentry at Manassas Industrial School and taught carpentry in the D.C. Vocational
School. He had married into the Houston family and lived in a
three-story brick town house next door to his wife's grandmother and aunt. Her first cousin was Charles Houston, the architect of the 1954 school desegregation law.

As we left our relatives and drove through town, Papa
stopped and bought fresh fish which was packed in ice and
wrapped in newspaper. For twenty-five cents he bought
enough to feed our family. He also bought a small stalk of bananas to take home for our special treat.

"Put on some clean clothes, we're going to Warrenton. Harold and I need haircuts. Your mother said she will stay home."
We were always excited to hear Papa say those words. We were
elated to go to Warrenton, a small town ten miles from our
home. The power structure prevented any growth in population. This was where my great grandmother Sally once lived and
where my grandfather was born. Surrounding the town were
vast horse farms of some of the wealthiest Americans: Sloans
(liniment heirs), Chryslers, Vanderbilts, and Randolphs, to
name a few. It was in the heart of the Hunt country. The rich
folks left their city mansions and gathered for their annual fox
hunt at some wealthy estate. They rode horses for the hunts. We
enjoyed our ride to Warrenton in Papa's 1926 Ford. This car had
a self-starter, which made it more luxurious than our previous
Ford, that had to be started by Papa cranking the engine by
hand. It was a touring car with a covered top and open sides. In
winter or during a rain the car was fitted with isinglass curtains
which snapped around the edge of the top and sides. Harold
usually rode up front with Papa when Mama was not with us.
We three girls rode in the backseat. This was a balmy day in June

and we basked in the warm breeze as the car moved down the road.

The road from our house was a sandy dirt road. It ended abruptly with a paved road when we entered Fauquier County. Due to its wealthy residents Fauquier was a richer county than Prince William County.

Several horse farms dotted the landscape with horses contained in green fields surrounded by white plank fences. Some were bred as race horses, some for trotting races and others were trained to be jumpers. The latter were used in the fox hunts; others performed in horse shows or race tracks owned by some wealthy businessmen. We were approaching the Bull Run Mountains which were covered by a blue haze. The series of mountains in front of this blue ridge were called the Blue Ridge Mountains.

The town of Warrenton was situated on seven small hills and was likened to the City of Rome. As we drove into the town we saw the area called Haiti where the colored lived. Negroes also owned small brick houses and their business buildings in town. Papa pointed to a small brick town house near the center of town that was once owned by Great Grandma Sally. Warrenton served as the Fauquier County seat where the wealthy sent their servants to shop for supplies. They also came in person for personal services. We usually went late in the afternoon and stayed after the black barber, Mr. Madison, closed his doors to the white clients. At that time Papa and Harold could get their hair cut. We visited Aunt Susie Dick's brother, Walter Clark, who had a cleaning establishment. Papa sneaked his Sunday blue serge suit to him to be cleaned; the rich white people did not allow colored people's clothes to be cleaned with theirs. We usually took our woolens to a black cleaner, Mr. Roy in Manassas.

The black druggist at the corner of the street where the Clarks lived also closed his doors to his white trade at 6:00 o'clock in the evening. Between the hours of six and seven, he allowed Papa to bring us in for an ice cream treat. I was impressed sitting at the small round marble table eating ice cream out of small glass bowls set in stainless steel holders.

The Clarks lived above their cleaning establishment. The shop was in a brick building that was on the street; a narrow sidewalk separated it from the street. One entered the building by two cement steps. Their quarters were a comfortable four room apartment. We called them Aunt and Uncle though they were not our blood kin.

"Uncle" Walt was a jolly stocky tan man. "Well, look who is here, Mack and his pretty girls and handsome son," he said.

"How have things been going with you, Walt?" Papa asked as he handed him the brown paper bag containing his suit.

"I'll have this ready before you leave this evening," Walt whispered. You will stay for dinner won't you? Go on up and see Violet."

We all went up to speak to "Aunt" Violet, an attractive, slender coffee colored woman. She periodically served as nursemaid to little Gloria Vanderbilt. She named her daughter Gloria who was born four months after Gloria Vanderbilt. That day she was keeping thee year old Gloria Vanderbilt while her mother was out of the country and her regular nursemaid had an emergency. Aunt Violet greeted us warmly.

Papa asked, "Violet, can I go to the A & P and get you something for dinner? Harold and I are getting haircuts and will be late going home."

"Get some hot dogs and buns. I have made a pot of vegetable soup," she answered. Hot dogs were our favorite food. We seldom ate them since the local country stores rarely stocked them due to lack of refrigeration. Aunt Violet requested that Eunice and I take the three girls down to the sidewalk and watch them while they took turns riding her daughter Gloria's tricycle. She said, "Gloria's nursemaid will pick her up before we have dinner."

Across the street from their home was the Warren Greene Hotel. This was the hotel where Great-Grandma Sally worked as a seamstress. It was here that she met the French chef, the father of her two sons. Southern cooking was not favored by the elite hotel guests.

I enjoyed watching the rich ladies in their finery sitting on the veranda. This was during the flapper era when women wore short dresses, rolled down stockings just below their knees and fancy headbands.

Wallace Warfield, who later became the Duchess of Windsor, was a resident at this hotel for several months in 1927 while waiting to divorce Warfield in order that she might marry Simpson. She could have been one of the guests I saw. After Aunt Violet served us dinner Papa took us for our ice cream treat, then drove us home, ending another perfect day.

Our parents always sheltered us from the indignities of segregation. We never felt deprived because we felt the power of their love. We sensed how deeply they cared that our self-esteem was never diminished.

When I compare the women and men in my two families, the Brown family women felt the need to be educated and self supporting. They had received superior education from a private institution. The Nickens wives were literate but most had not received formal higher education beyond the seventh grade. They enjoyed their dependence on their husbands and accepted their subservient roles in the family. I conclude that the dominant role the Nickens men held in their family was the result of experiencing freedom over several generations.

Both families maintained high family and moral values. There was no evidence of illegitimacy in three generations. They exhibited restraint and self discipline. Using profanity was taboo. The only expletive I ever heard my father use was, "Oh the dog's foot" or "Doggone". There is no history of crime or poverty in either family. All the Nickens marriages survived. Once a

Nickens uncle went to his mother to discuss a problem in his marriage. She told him, "Go home and work it out; no Nickens man has ever left his wife and family." There existed an intense emotional dependency between the mother and child. They nursed their children until the arrival of the next child. The Nickens family always appeared calm and relaxed. The women in the Brown family were controlling and domineering which caused much conflict with their husbands. Mama and her sister Mamie were the exceptions.

Early in life I was puzzled as to why Grandma Brown was so distant and resentful toward Grandpa. He was frugal and one might say stingy, but he was not a mean man. She always referred to him as "the old man". They were in their late sixties when I stayed with them, yet I sensed their separateness. I am inclined to believe she resented the fact he had been a field slave and retained some of the slave culture while she had lived in the back of the big house with her slave mother and did not associate with the field slaves.

Consequently, my maternal grandparents had a stormy marriage resulting in my grandmother's leaving and staying with a sister in Philadelphia for several months. It was never made clear to me what caused the conflict, but I surmise it had to do with each wanting control in the relationship. Uncle Franklin was guilty of physical spousal abuse. He eventually divorced. My Aunt Marie and her husband had a volatile relationship. There were occasions when their older child came and got my grandmother to quell the disturbance.

I have theorized that my maternal grandparents experienced more trauma, deprivation, and repression of their anger against the white master and eventually white employee. Also Grandpa was for the first time experiencing the role of male authority in a family.

Frazier the sociologist writes:
> During the slave era and post-slave era the woman
> played the dominant role in the family and marriage
> relations. These women had doubtless been schooled
> in self-reliance and self-sufficiency during slavery.
> Neither economic necessity nor tradition had instilled
> a spirit of subordination to masculine authority.

My mother was a child born between two tempestuous sisters. She acquired a passive persona because she could not tolerate confrontation.

Two in the Nickens family, Fred and Katie, married into the Colvin family making their offspring double first cousins. Another brother married a Colvin cousin. These two families are so interrelated I feel compelled to include some of their family's histories in my family memoirs. The patriarch, George Colvin, was in my grandfather's generation. We all called him "Papa George." His mother was a mulatto free woman named Mary Preston. His father was James Colvin, a white man who lived nearby in Catlett. This Colvin family were rich farmers and owned a vast crop farm. They did not own slaves. James and Mary had a long love relationship. He allowed their son to carry his last name; thus, all his descendants bore the last name, Colvin. Both families lived in the vicinity known as Greenville. The Tapscot and Grigsby families also lived in the area. The Colvins, Tapscots, and Grigsbys were predominantly Caucasian with a tint of Negro and Indian mixture. These four families formed an enclave isolated from the general black communities. All four families adhered to perpetuating the color line. Every descendant ranged in color from Caucasian to light brown skin. They propagated a distinct race of Americans with straight to wavy hair and blond to black hair color. Due to my Grandfather Brown's black ancestry my mother's family ranged from olive to light brown skin and hair from straight to extremely curly. These families from both communities were conservative in their church worship services with the exception of my maternal grandfather. They did not hire ministers who preached highly emotional sermons, rejecting the culture of blacks who behaved differently. My Grandfather Brown attended a sanctified church that had services similar to the old slave religious rites held in the bushes.

As I became older I grew to understand why he was drawn to this church; that was the way he worshipped with the slaves as a child in Alabama.

I frequently spent some weeks staying with my paternal grandparents and paternal aunts. I observed they were very patient and affectionate with their children and grandchildren. Grandpa used to hold me on his lap and talk to me. I never saw them whip any child. I often wondered why they were jovial and lighthearted when my Grandfather Brown was a distant, morose individual; and why my mother whipped us and her sister Louise whipped her students.

In studying the history of slave practices I learned that slaves whipped their children to make them bend to authority and to spare them from the Master's or overseer's whips which would leave them scarred for life. They refrained from being affectionate parents to lessen the grief they felt when they or their children were sold and separated. Their disciplinary and child rearing practices were passed down to the next generation. I have often asked myself, was this the reason for the difference in the way my parents related to us as children? Was it because my father came from a family that for generations had been free while my mother was reared by parents who were born slaves?

Each summer when our Aunt Geneva came from Washington to spend time at Ringwood and bring her children we had a family reunion at Grandpa's. There would be as many as sixty people gathered spanning three generations. Each cousin had someone her or his own age to play with. We played games appropriate for our age levels. The men played croquet and held horse shoe pitching contests. The women prepared the food and tables and talked about their pregnancies and children. They tended their babies and toddlers while the children and men played.

We ate in shifts; the youngest age group ate first, then the teens and young adults while the men ate separately in the dinning room. The women waited on each group and ate last holding their babies. At one time my siblings and I had ninety-two living first cousins, fifty-eight on my father's side and thirty-four on my mother's side of the family.

In addition to our summer family day we attended the family birthdays at which time my father and his brothers furnished the music. Each one played a musical instrument by ear. Dick and Cook played the fiddle, French the guitar and Papa played the banjo as the children and grownups danced. Macon called the figures for the square dancing between waltzes.

A family reunion was held at my mother's parents' home each summer when Mama's sister, Lavinia, visited from New Jersey. She was held in high esteem in the family. She had attended schools in D.C. and worked in the federal government. While there, she met and married a physician, Dr. Lawrence Brown. They moved to Elizabeth, New Jersey, where he practiced medicine. She was a sophisticated lady, always dressed in fine clothes, lived in a beautiful home and drove a luxury car. She played bridge and tennis.

Although we were enthralled by her visits and happy to spend a day with our cousins, the day was not as fun-filled as the Nickens gatherings. My aunts complained about their lives and marriages. Their neuroses were reflected in their children's behavior. Grandpa placed restrictions that kept the children from being free as we would have liked.

Some authorities state that it takes four generations to produce a leisure class. The Nickens family members in my father's generation reaped the benefit of their father's thriftiness, business acumen, inherited wealth and land holdings. Having been free for several generations and economically independent, they were people who enjoyed leisure. They were musicians, hunters, card and game players, and horsemen. They were gregarious and enjoyed socializing. Since all their basic needs were met without the necessity of hard labor, they did not feel the need for higher education. Despite having grown up in Washington which provided free education through senior high school, only three completed high school—my father, his sister Geneva and Uncle Cook. The wives never worked outside of the home. They had large families and remained housewives who concentrated on rearing their children. This lifestyle produced some stagnation. When the great Depression occurred their small business ventures failed, the banks closed causing Grandpa to lose money, large farming cooperatives had formed and small scale farming was no longer profitable.

Those that remained in Virginia with large families could not afford to send their children to a private high school. It was not until 1938, when Virginia consolidated their schools and made Manassas Industrial High School a public high school that the younger Nickens children were enabled to receive a high school education.

Some family members moved to D.C. where jobs were more available. My uncles Macon, Fred and Aunt Katie's husband Felix began working for a wealthy white man by the name of Groom. Macon was a chauffeur, French the butler, and Felix groomed the horses. On occasions when the owners were away we would visit the big house. We had to enter from the rear door.

The property was eventually sold in the '60s. The new owner made it a "Think Tank" where the State Department and other high-level agencies and businesses held conferences. He named it Airlee House. As a professional educator, I was invited to attend a conference being held there in 1969. This time I was ushered in the front entrance by servants carrying my bags. This time I was awakened in the morning and given the morning paper. No television, radios nor alarm clocks were allowed. This time I went down to the plantation breakfast served by a crew of men in white coats. I had progressed and the State of Virginia had progressed.

In comparing the two families, because my maternal grandparents were forced to work excessively hard to acquire their land, build their home and educate their children, there was no time for fun and games. The Brown descendants were more educated and married successful mates; they had a higher economic status than the Nickens at one time. The daughters that worked used their money to enlarge their parents' home into an attractive farm house.

Our family remained close to the Colvins all my life. In 1976 a Nickens-Colvin family reunion was held on the property of one of the Nickens-Colvin descendants. This reunion has been held annually since its inception. I had the opportunity to attend the 1994 reunion which is held during two days. The opening ceremonies began with a prayer by a Nickens deacon in the Greenville Church. The rest of the day was spent visiting and conversing with relatives, sharing food, games, racing contests and a hayride. Some went to the Church nearby and visited the graveyard that contains the graves of our deceased relatives. At this reunion my brother was officially recognized as the patriarch of the Nickens family.

It is important for one to understand why these rural Virginia families were compelled to retain their mulatto physical characteristics. Colorism or light skin versus dark skin dates back to Colonial Virginia. Historians write that from the time the first blacks arrived in 1619 sexual relations between whites, blacks and Indians were prevalent. Many interracial marriages were legalized until the statute of 1705 which prohibited such marriages. These unions produced a large mulatto population in the colony. Many of these mulattoes were free before the slave act of 1680 having served as indentured servants; consequently they enjoyed some economic and social advantages over slaves arriving from Africa.

The free persons of color were forbidden to fraternize with slaves for fear of inciting a slave insurrection; thus, free mulattoes married other free mulattoes. This lessened the chances of marriage for free women of color who often became mistresses of their white employers and bore their children (such was the case of my great grandmother, Sally). This was a ploy by the white establishment to keep the Negro race divided.

At the beginning of the nineteenth century, Virginia became the largest slave trading state in the Union. Virginia planters found that selling slaves proved to be more profitable than supporting them. When cotton became "king" in the deep southern states as a result of the invention of the cotton gin, many slaves were sold to the cotton plantation owners. (This was the cause of my Grandfather Brown and his sister being sold.)

Dark-skinned, free Negroes were often kidnapped by the slave traders, robbed of their freedom papers and sold as slaves. It was more difficult to prove a free mulatto was a slave; therefore it became imperative for a mulatto free mother to retain her children's mulatto physical appearance.

During the slave era, many white masters sired children of their slave women, producing mulattoes. In most instances these women and their children were the house slaves who lived in their master's house and were discouraged from association with the field slaves. They acquired the language and assimilated the culture of their white owners. When they were freed, they were allowed to continue to remain in the household and work for pay. (My maternal great grandmother had two children by her former master after she was freed.)

By contrast when the field slaves were freed, most were turned off the farms and deprived of any means of making a living; they roamed the countryside stealing in order to exist. Their family structure had been dissolved by their slave masters who broke up family units when they sold some family members down south. No moral codes governed their behavior, whereas the former house slaves emulated their owner's demeanor and family values.

These two families, the Nickens and Browns, constituted an upper social class more or less isolated from the majority of the rural black population. They shut themselves away from the general population in order not to be overwhelmed by the flood of immorality surrounding them. The light skin mulattoes continued the practice of marrying other mulattoes of mixed blood, producing mulatto children.

They finally came into the mainstream of black culture during World War II. The men were drafted and saw what the rest of the world was like. There is now more worldliness, a more relatedness, an understanding of the needs of other people. They now feel free to select mates regardless of the color of their skin and the texture of their hair.

Chapter Six

Our Virginia Communities

Of the four villages that surrounded our property prior to the 1960's, three were populated exclusively by whites: Gainesville, Haymarket, and Buckland. The residents in the Thoroughfare vicinity were mostly black with a few whites.

Originally a large section of Thoroughfare was a part of Cloverland Plantation which was owned by a man named Chew. His first son, whom he named Primas from the Latin word meaning first, was by a slave. When their son reached the age of eighteen he freed him and deeded a large parcel of land to him from the Cloverland Plantation. This son took Primas for his last name. The Primas heirs sold acreage lots to other blacks who were freed after 1863 and who had acquired money by being employed on the plantations that were located near Cloverland.

Several of my mother's relatives bought property from former plantation owners whose land abutted Cloverland and settled in the Thoroughfare vicinity. My grandparents and my grandmother's brother, Milton Barbour, bought adjoining properties containing forty acres each. My grandmother's half sister Mariah married Thomas Primas, one of the Primas heirs who inherited a large farm. Her sister also owned property in the area. My grandmother's half brother John bought a five acre parcel in the area. Another of Grandma's half sisters who married a Harris bought acreage in the vicinity.

In the early nineteen hundreds Mama's sister Louise and her husband, Frank Allen, bought forty acres off the Forkland farm across the road from Grandpa's farm. Three of my mother's first cousins, the Berry Brothers, acquired a two hundred acre farm in the area. They were progressive farmers and accumulated a fair amount of wealth. They built a four story mansion on the property where many city folks stayed on their visits. The house and the surrounding grounds became a gathering place for people from the city and from the community.

Eight other black families owned property in the area. Being early landowners the residents developed a progressive and prosperous community. They built comfortable houses on their properties. A two room school named North Fork after a nearby stream was built by the colored community for colored children in 1884 and continued as such until 1936. A church was built in 1865 and named Oakrum Baptist Church. There were two stores, one owned by blacks and the other owned by whites. A hall which served as a community center was built by The Odd Fellows, a black mutual aid society that provided help for families in sickness and death.

Most of the residents were of a racial mixture about three generations from their white heritage. One resident, Mr. Allen, was Indian. There was one exception, a Johnson family, whose members were dark skinned. One side of the family assimilated with the culture of the community. The other family did not conform to the laws and were considered "low class blacks" by the other residents. Violence often erupted in their home. Except for that one family the black residents were extremely conservative and adhered strictly to behavior codes set by the church. Social dancing, gambling, adultery and bearing a child out of wedlock were forbidden. These people spoke with perfect diction; their speech patterns reflected close association with upperclass whites leading me to believe their ancestors were originally house slaves. They aspired to emulate the manners, style and culture of their former white masters. Their social dancing however consisted of folk dances handed down from slaves in former days, reflecting the call and response pattern.

Social and fund raising affairs were held in the Odd Fellows' Hall. Families brought food to sell; fried chicken, ham sandwiches, potato salad, homemade ice cream and cakes were usual food items. Bottles of soda pop purchased from stores were sold for a profit. The only social contact between single males and females acceptable were two arm holding games, "Little Liza Jane" and "Julia Ann". These folk dances allowed partners to lock arms and strut around when their turn was called by the lead singer. Sometimes they selected partners and marched around the hall singing, with locked arms. At the end each man escorted his partner to the table and treated her to her choice of food. The older married couples sat on the side with their younger children and chaperoned.

Another colored community located four miles from our house was called "The Settlement". This area was one mile south of the Gainesville village. The area originally was part of the Tyler Plantation. A road ran through the area we called "The Lane". The slave quarters were formerly located on this lane. These slaves were the field slaves. A Tyler daughter was heir to this part of the plantation. One of the Tyler sons, whose name was Steve, lived with a free woman of color in a house at the end of The Lane. He was considered a family outcast. Despite not legally owning the property he sold lots along this slave row to the freed slaves for five dollars each. When the sister learned what the brother had done she reimbursed the former slaves and gave them legal deeds to the property they had purchased.

A son was conceived from the union of Steve and his colored mistress. The boy bore his father's name, Steve Tyler. His family lived in a comfortable house at the end of The Lane. The other houses were three and four room sub-standard homes built and occupied by these former slaves. The lots were just large enough for a small vegetable garden. I was astonished when I accompanied my mother on one of her visits to a pupil's home and observed that the floor of the house consisted of hard-packed dirt.

A white family by the name of McRae donated a building to be used as a school for the colored children in this community in 1870, the year Virginia first began public education. In 1888 the school was located in a building in the center of the town of Gainesville. It was moved in 1907 to a hall belonging to the colored church. In 1914 a new two room school was built on an acre of ground on Lee Highway. This was the school where my parents taught and where I attended from the first through the fifth grades.

The church named Mt. Pleasant Baptist Church was built by the colored residents in 1875. A hall was also built on Church property. Other financially stable families bought property surrounding The Lane and built standard country homes. Most of these families functioned as a close family unit and led highly traditional moral lives following the rules as set forth by the church.

Other residents who occupied The Lane and some who owned property near The Lane were less organized, dysfunctional families whose moral delinquencies were frowned on by the church and other residents. The men and a few women were prone to violent acts against one another. Many of the families had maternal households. Illegitimacy rate was high. Several men were jailed, usually for an act of violence. Their economic survival depended many times on outwitting the white man or committing acts just outside the law. The young women were frequently brought before the Church at the Deacons Quarterly Meetings to face charges of immoral conduct for having a baby out of wedlock or for some other transgression. They were readmitted to the Church the next month after "begging the Deacon's pardon".

The effectiveness of the Church in this community was not as strong as the Thoroughfare Oakrum Baptist Church.

Frazier writes:

> The effectiveness of the church as an institution of control over sex behavior is dependent upon the characteristic of the family life and other social relations in these communities. In the better organized communities where the church and other forms of communal enterprises are supported by families with some property and traditions of regular family life, the church reflects the character of its constituents and in turn controls to some extent their behavior.

After researching the history of the Settlement and reading sociological references written about black families, I can now understand the causes of the contrasting modes of behavior of the Settlement residents as opposed to the Thoroughfare residents.

Reminiscing on those years I spent attending McRae School and my parents' contact with the folksy and colorful characters in the Settlement left me with many memories. Each school day I would ride with my parents to school. As we approached the Settlement we came to Mrs. Nanny McPherson's house. On Monday mornings we would hear, "Mr. Mack! Mr. Mack!" That would be Miss Nanny running down the path that sloped to the road. She served as the town crier, informing Papa of the happenings that went on in the Settlement during the weekend. In warm weather she had bare feet and wore a net over her hair; her fair skinned cheeks were heavily rouged. She was usually attired in a fancy blouse and wide skirt.

Papa would stop the car and she would divulge who got cut or shot, or what girl was now pregnant and who the father was. One morning she excitedly reported the shooting of a girl, Pauline, that was visiting the Brooks family. "Old Bob shot her because she refused to do the nasty with him. Shot her right in the groin. They are taking her to the station now and putting her on the train to go back to Washington for medical treatment." As we drove down the road we spotted two men driving a horse drawn wagon. Pauline was lying on a mattress in the wagon and covered by a quilt. A man and a woman walked behind the wagon. That incident was never reported to the law and Bob was never punished. The Settlement people were afraid of him. He was a mean man without a conscience.

Throughout the years she reported other traumatic incidents. Lena Tyler was burned to death while pouring gasoline, trying to light a fire. A Harris man shot and killed a sheriff who was called by his wife's father for beating and threatening to kill her. He was tried and later electrocuted. There was an incident concerning Nat Peterson who was a "bad egg" and had one ear, the other having been shot off during an altercation. The white sheriff had been summoned to quell a shooting taking place between Nat and a man from Catharpen. The man hid behind the Sheriff's horse and in aiming at the man Nat shot and killed the Sheriff's horse. Nat went to prison for several years for that offense.

As we drove toward the school the Robinson children would be standing on the road waiting to wave and speak to us. "Good mawn-awning, Mister Nickens. Good mawn-awning, Miz Nickens". Their voices had a quiver and they would stretch out the middle syllables of words.

On the left side of the road was the Church; across the road from the Church was Mrs. Mary McPherson's home. She was always called Miz Plummy by the colored community. (Mrs. was always pronounced "Miz".) Miz Plummy was a stout tan colored woman. She was the most enterprising person in the area. In addition to being Church Mother, the person responsible for keeping and cleaning the communion sacraments, she was also the mid wife, whiskey supplier (prohibition was enforced) and numbers runner. She commuted to D.C. daily on the bus and turned in the residents' numbers to the dealer. At that time playing numbers was illegal.

When we arrived at the School, Papa made fires in the stoves while Mama prepared her lessons for the day. Mama was an innovative and creative teacher. She taught by doing and seeing although she never read Dewey's *Methods of Teaching*. She would take us to the stream in back of the school and teach geography by having us observe water and land forms. We learned mathematical concepts by using acorns we would gather and keep in a box for our Arithmetic classes. We made alphabet books and phonics books, making houses for the "at family" or the "ing family", etc.

Papa's upper grade classes would join the lower grade classes for morning devotionals which consisted of Papa or Mama reading a part of the Bible, singing a hymn and reciting the Lord's Prayer. We stood and said the "Flag Salute" at the end.

A mixture of odors permeated the classroom: kerosene and cooking odors in the wraps; chalk dust, food odors from lunch pails and a faint smell of urine. The dark skinned children's faces were greased with vaseline or lard to keep from looking ashy. The girls wore their hair in tiny cornrowed braids or twisted and parted and wound with a cord string. A water cooler sat on a back table and each family had a tin cup with their last name pasted on it. The water was drawn from a pump in the school yard.

Occasionally Miss Anna McKinney would be at school waiting to report some child who fought one of her children. She had nine illegitimate children including a set of twins. One child was by the white banker in Haymarket for whom she worked. She was a slender dark skinned woman who always wore her head tied up in a white cloth. Her usual complaint was, "These chilluns are always pickin on my chillun. You know my chillun

ain't got no father." A fact that was well known in the neighborhood.

Papa joined Mt. Pleasant Church and served as a deacon.
One evening he announced he was going to the Deacon's meeting because they planned to put Miz Plummy out of church for
selling whiskey in her home across from the church. When he
returned he reported what had happened. Miz Plummy
brought her daughter Annie with her. After the charge was
made she got up and told them what part of her anatomy they
could kiss. Annie patted her behind and yelled, "And mine too."
They then left the church.

Tom Watson, a burly man who remained a bachelor, was the
stud in the neighborhood. Three children from different families
were whispered to be fathered by him. He lived with his mother
in a new house he had built. In spite of his ramblings he was an
upright citizen and had the respect of the community. Several
years later after his mother's death his house was burned during
the night with him in it. His body was found the next day among
the ashes. Some people always said he was murdered, but no
one was charged. Many humorous stories were told about the
people of the Settlement; others were tales of pathos.

After Papa joined Mt. Pleasant Church and became deacon
most of our church attendance was there. A Reverend Strother
was the pastor of that church and three other churches. Church
was held once a month in each area. He was a dramatic preacher
with his sermons reaching a crescendo and whispering at the
end. One warm Sunday a lady member got happy and fell out in
the aisle. Her dress flew up as she fell revealing scanty undies.
The minister had a good bird's eye view from the pulpit. Some
deacons went to pick her up, but the pastor said, "Let her be,
brothers. Let her lay where God flung her."

After Reverend Strother's death a new minister, Reverend
Garland from Richmond, was appointed. He was mostly white
with blond hair and blue eyes. There was some relationship

between him and an elderly lady in the community named Mrs. Berry. People whispered that he was the child of one of her female relatives, and was fathered by a white man. He came once a month and usually stayed a week with this relative. Sometimes his wife accompanied him. She played the organ well, a relief from the playing of Miss Ruth Berry, who made many mistakes. After two years of Reverend Garland's serving as minister, a young single Negroid looking woman came to church with a little fair blue eyed baby. She was brought up and charged at the Deacon's meeting for having an illegitimate child and expelled from church. She was readmitted the next month after "begging the Deacon's pardon". It was whispered around that she admitted the minister was the father.

Mr. Steve Tyler was another colorful character in the community. He was a large rotund white looking man. He made a living by gathering fruit from the orchards and vegetables and selling them to the white people in the area. One day he had a load of apples on his truck and stopped by a white woman's house. She asked to buy a barrel full. He told her to go to her house and he would fill her barrel. He turned the barrel upside down and piled apples on the bottom, which made the barrel appear full. After resting on his truck for half an hour, he called the woman to come out and see how he had piled the apples filling the barrel over the brim. She paid him and he drove off in his truck. He and his wife, a genteel lady, had eight children. A son and two daughters still lived at home. His two daughters were sophisticated for the area at that time. They were good looking and wore riding pants and smoked cigarettes. His daughter Lena, was the one that was burned to death. Four of his grandchildren attended McRae School with me. Mama selected his granddaughter Sylvia for my friend and playmate. Her younger sister Edith was fiery. On three occasions during my attendance the whole school became angry with me because Papa or Mama had punished a family member. They would put Edith up to fight me. I was proud of the way I defended myself. Once I left marks on her face when I scratched her. My parents would hear the commotion and immediately stop the fight. We were both kept in for fighting. Mama told me later it was not to punish me but to protect me until the pupils' anger subsided.

The county attempted to provide a health program. Dr. Williams, the black doctor from Manassas, came periodically to vaccinate for small pox and inoculate for diphtheria and whooping cough. He also examined for physical defects. The county awarded a five star certificate to the student whose defects were corrected. My parents took me to the dentist and had all my cavities filled in one day. I was the only pupil who received a certificate.

Mama would send to the *Normal Instructor Magazine* and get free samples of Colgate toothpaste and Lifebouy soap, enough to pass out to each child. She truly cared for her charges. One day a student's house burned to the ground. Nothing was saved. She had only the clothes she wore to school that day. Mama bought two different yards of fabric and stayed up late two evenings making new dresses which she gave to this girl. She also bought new underwear for her.

The only school supplies provided by the county were two boxes containing chalk, a large dictionary, two erasers, and two maps. The teachers were given a roll book in which they kept attendance and submitted to the Superintendent at the end of the school term. The parents had to buy their children's books, tablet, and pencils at a great financial sacrifice. The books were passed down in the families as they completed their grade levels. To prevent the books from becoming too worn and soiled Mama sent to the *Normal Instructor* for book covers and there was a book covering session each year. My parents swept and cleaned their classrooms after school.

Rachael Berry, the wife of one of Mama's cousins, was the county school coordinator. She came to the school periodically and taught health education and industrial arts. She also organized "Home Maker" clubs among the women in the communities. One year she held an oratorical contest among the children in the Thoroughfare community. I won by speaking a poem about a bumblebee and a rose. I was six years old at the time.

Virginia began building The Lee Highway in 1926 which is now Route 211. The school was situated on this road. Convicts from a chain gang worked on the road. The men in the Settlement were deprived of getting labor jobs working on this road. During the construction which took two years, instruction in the school would be interrupted. The engineer would come to school and advise the teachers to take the children a good distance away from the school because they were blasting rock. One morning when we arrived a huge boulder had come through the roof of the school and left a gaping hole in the ceiling. Papa notified the superintendent who came and inspected it. It was six weeks before the hole was repaired. It was not until Roosevelt began WPA and other workfare programs that young people were able to get laboring jobs other than farm labor.

Disease, accidents and violent acts took their toll on the Settlement community. Several people died of tuberculosis. One was the Robinson children's mother. George Johnson from Thoroughfare was shot through the head; the bullet penetrated one side and went out the other. He lived and suffered no ill effects. He was looked upon as a "miracle man". George got religion after that incident and became a law abiding citizen.

Mama brought Helen, my cousin to school with us. I was happy to have her to play with. She was always my closest friend. She attended two years with me. She brought my sister Elizabeth to school when she became four years old that year. Papa taught me in the fourth and fifth grades. After I completed the fifth grade, Mama entered me in the sixth grade in North Fork School in Thoroughfare where my cousin Evelyn Primas was my teacher. Later that year I went to D.C. and had little contact with the Settlement people after that.

Miz Plummy died in 1953. In retrospect, she was the most memorable woman with whom our family had contact in the Settlement. Her retort to the minister and some deacons whom she knew to be hypocritically pious was justified since they were attempting to deprive her of a source of income. She was the matriarch of the community to whom the Settlement people turned for medicinal cures, loans when in financial straits, and sage advice.

Her husband worked in D.C.; therefore, she had the task of rearing her children and supplementing her family's income. She also reared some grandchildren. When I last saw her, she was on the Greyhound bus holding a grandbaby, going to the city to take numbers and collect the money for the lucky ones who hit. The two activities that she operated outside the law eventually became legal.

I recently talked with one of her grandsons who related more information regarding her. He mentioned her generosity. He described situations when the family was eating at the dinner table and a child or woman neighbor would come to her house and inform her there was nothing to eat in their house. Miz Plummy would take part of her dinner from the table and give it to that person to take home.

Her skills as a midwife were well known. When a woman in labor called Dr. Payne, the white doctor, he would tell them, "Let Mary do it; she is better than I am." His other reason was he knew he would not be paid in cash. On the other hand, Miz Plummy would return home after a delivery with a ham or chicken, and other foodstuffs instead of cash.

A survey was made one year of the doctors who had delivered the most babies in Prince William County. Dr. Williams, the colored doctor, was honored for delivering the most babies; however, Miz Plummy was acknowledged as having delivered the largest number of babies. She only lost one mother from childbirth.

Her grandson tells of the time she got on a bus which stopped when she waved it down. She sat in the front seat. The driver did not ask her to move but later stopped further down the road where the sheriff was stationed. The bus driver demanded that the sheriff make Miz Plummy go to the back. The sheriff looked at the passengers seated and remarked, "There is no seat available for her to sit. I will not make this woman move. She brought me into this world." Miz Plummy continued her trip to Washington in the front seat.

Now as I reflect on the Settlement families from The Lane and their mores, there were many positive aspects in their family and behavior patterns. The mothers had a strong attachment to their children and worked hard to fulfill their basic needs. They took pride in their children's appearance when they sent them to school. They received no outside financial help or charity. The welfare program did not exist. The grandmothers played an important role in keeping their families together; the children respected and honored them. A few fathers were able to assume the authority role in the family, but many had to leave their families and seek work in cities.

The young adult males were the most victimized ones of the oppressed society. They were prevented from working on jobs that paid enough for them to marry, build a home and raise their families. Much of the violence was caused by consuming bad alcohol. They suppressed their rage during the week when they worked as laborers under the white man's rule and resorted to drinking on weekends.

All the men and women held my parents in the highest esteem and treated them with utmost respect. A case in point—my father was the referee for the ball games between the teams from various nearby communities. The games could have been explosive situations. However, every player accepted my father's call. They looked upon him as being infallible.

When the Manassas Industrial School became a regional school in 1938, the Settlement students were transported by bus, enabling them to receive a high school education. This third generation were financially able to buy cars and commute to areas that provided better jobs. During the Second World War, some men were drafted and served in the military. Jobs became more plentiful as large businesses later located nearby.

The fourth generation have made the Settlement a viable community. Many have retired from their civil service jobs in Washington and returned to the area where they have built attractive homes. Two of Miz Plummy's grandsons, our second cousins, live in two well kept homes near our Virginia home on lots that were formerly part of Uncle Dick's property.

The church has been modernized and enlarged; it serves as a community center in addition to a place of worship. The same pattern of growth has evolved in the Thoroughfare Community.

Chapter Seven

Manassas Industrial School

The Manassas Industrial School was not only a source of secondary education, it was a seat of culture and served as a community center for the African-Americans who were residents of northern Virginia.

Our family attended piano recitals and exhibitions of crafts from various elementary schools in Prince William County that were on display at this school. We attended graduation exercises that were held on Memorial Day. On that day we observed exhibits of samples of the students' work. In the morning session we picnicked on the Campus lawn, greeting old friends and meeting the faculty members.

The graduation exercises took place in the afternoon in a grove-like setting. The seats were built on a sloping hill with the stage at the bottom. This seat arrangement gave everyone a good view of the stage. At these programs we heard the school choir render classical compositions. The speakers were usually some well-known national figure or orator. My mother, her two sisters and her two brothers were alumni. My sister Eunice attended the school one year and my brother Harold attended two years. All of my cousins who lived in the town of Manassas received their secondary education at this institution.

My parents attended summer sessions that provided in-service training for teachers, a criteria for renewing their teacher certificates.

Manassas Industrial School was founded by Jennie Dean, a former slave, and chartered in 1893. The school was located on a farm comprising two-hundred acres of land one mile from the town of Manassas. At the time she began her mission, there were no schools in northern Virginia that provided secondary education for colored youth. It remained a private institution until 1938.

A quote from the charter states:

> The school was established ultimately and primarily to improve the moral and intellectual condition of Negro youth placed under its care and influence.

The charter further states:

> . . . that the students would receive such instructions in the common English branches, the Mechanical Arts and trades in farming, housework, needlework and other occupation. . . that shall be practical and also useful in enabling the said youth to earn a livelihood.

Miss Dean developed a strong influence in the community and the people received with confidence anything she told them. She called a number of parents in the community and exhorted them:

> Keep your children at home. Don't send them to cities. You must buy your lands; become taxpayers. Make all you can. Meanwhile, I will go out and raise the money to build a school where your children can be educated to trades. You do your part and I will do mine.

She was able to accomplish her dream by forming a bi-racial base of local support in the late 19th century, and used her diplomatic skills and powers of persuasion to obtain large sums of money for the school from northern philanthropists.

In October of 1884 the school opened in the farm dwelling house with six pupils attending. The instructors gave free their first year of work, receiving only their board in return.

Later the campus contained two dormitory buildings and an administration building which housed offices, classrooms, a library and an auditorium. A large barn was constructed on the farm area. This farm was used to teach agricultural skills and as a source for providing food for the boarding students and faculty. A hospital, laundry and a home for the principal and one for a faculty member were built. From a school population of six the school eventually averaged one hundred fifty students per year.

During the 1920's and 30's the school was beset by financial problems. Due to the mounting financial burdens on the school and following much negotiation between officials of the school and surrounding counties, the Manassas Industrial School was transferred to the counties of Prince William, Fairfax and Fauquier. In 1938 it became the Manassas Regional High School with these counties providing bus transportation for the students. From 1938 to 1954 the Manassas Regional High School was the only secondary school for the people of color in northern Virginia.

My mother's sister, Marie, was the first family member to graduate from the original school in 1901. She received an appointment teaching in a one-room school in Delaware, a community of mixed race families of Native American, Caucasian and African Americans. She was required to send a picture and her color and physical features met the qualifications specified by that community. After a three-year teaching stint she left her job to marry and live in Manassas. My mother was appointed to fill the vacancy and taught in this Delaware community for three years.

The Manassas school was razed in 1960. My sister, Elizabeth, served on the Manassas Museum Black Heritage Preservation Foundation which was instrumental in making the original

school site the Jenny Dean Memorial Park. The park was dedicated in June, 1995.

Chapter Eight

Eyes on the Prize

*It is not your environment, it is you—the quality of your
minds, the integrity of your souls, and the determination of
your will, that will decide your future and shape your lives.*

—Benjamin C. Mays

In May of 1927 when I went to the mailbox for the newspaper, large headlines stood out in bold print, LINDBERGH COMPLETES TRANSATLANTIC FLIGHT. This news elicited lengthy discussions at the dinner table.

At that time I had seen only one airplane. A man used to fly from the Manassas Airport and land in a field near Thoroughfare School. The pupils were allowed to go see the plane up close and talk to the pilot. His name was "Billy" Mitchell, the early advocate of air power.

Other changes were occurring in my family at this time. Papa bought a truck that summer and began a summer huckstering business. Mama had learned to drive the 1926 Model A Ford that Papa had bought new the previous year. Eunice entered Manassas Industrial School in the eighth grade where Harold was a high school freshman. Aunt Estelle stopped caring for Elizabeth because of failing health and Grandma Brown kept her during the school week until Mama and Papa returned from teaching at McRae School where Papa taught me in the fifth grade.

We were all proud of Harold at his eighth grade graduation. He was the valedictorian of his class. He was smaller in size than the average student; therefore, he did not go out for the athletic teams. He never grew over five feet seven, and remained small in stature.

I missed my sister and brother that year. The music teacher at the school informed my parents that Eunice displayed talent as a pianist. By the time they came home from school that summer, Papa had bought a piano.

That fall Mama cried often. I surmised she was missing not having all her family home. One weekend Papa's cousin Fanny and her husband visited us. Saturday morning while the men had gone hunting, Cousin Fanny sat in our kitchen to visit with Mama as she cooked breakfast. I observed that Mama had been crying softly all morning.

Cousin Fanny asked, "Susie, do you want to tell me what is wrong?"

Mama sobbed, "I want my children to have a college education and I don't see any way we can manage it."

Cousin Fanny said, "Pray on it and you will find a way."

At the end of the summer Mr. and Mrs. Madden, who were friends of our family, came to visit us from their home in Washington, D.C. Mrs. Madden asked my parents to let Eunice stay with them and attend the D.C. schools. In return for her room and board, she could help with light housework.

My parents said they would give it some thought. It was too late for her to transfer immediately so she returned to Manassas for the first semester. They decided to accept Mrs. Madden's offer and allow both Eunice and Harold to go to Washington for the beginning of the second semester. Harold was to stay with Mama's brother Franklin and his wife while Eunice stayed with the Maddens.

The Nickens-Colvin family reunion

The fall of 1928 Papa learned he had been transferred to a school in Catharpin as a penalty for driving around the county urging the colored people to vote against a proposed school bond to build a modern school for the white children. Aunt Louise was fired from her teaching job for taking similar action.

The bond proposal was voted down and the whites attributed its failure to pass to Papa and Aunt Louise who were most vocal. No money was proposed to improve the colored schools.

The evening he received the letter, Papa sat at the dinner table and gave us a profound lecture. He sensed our bewilderment.

"Don't worry," he assured us. "I will drive the truck to Catharpin School and Mama can drive to her school. At the end of the school year I will resign my teaching job and huckster full time." Then he added, "I urged colored people to vote against this bond because it would raise our taxes yet not improve the colored schools. Now the whites see that the colored people can stop their proposals by voting against them. This may make them provide better schools for our children and school buses to take them to school."

Five years later what he predicted became a reality. School buses were provided for colored children and a modern brick school was eventually built that served black children from three communities.

Both of my parents valued their voting privilege. That year Al Smith was running for president against Herbert Hoover. The colored people always voted Republican because that party freed the slaves. This election Papa decided to vote for Al Smith because he felt he would do more for the colored people in the country. The whites were against Smith because he was Catholic and indicated they feared the Pope would be running the country.

My parents paid their poll tax and Papa put a tag on his car that read, "Vote for Al Smith." Al Smith lost the election and Hoover became President.

That fall I entered the sixth grade at North Fork School in Thoroughfare where my cousin, Evelyn Primas taught. The population of the community had diminished, because of families moving to cities to get jobs; it was presently a one-room school. The school was two miles from our home.

I would walk to school by myself and sometimes with my cousin, Helen. I was just starting to be aware of the beauties of nature. The foliage was in its full splendor by October. A drought had occurred the previous year but the rains of the past spring helped Virginia to retain its reputation as one of the most beautiful spots in the country. After passing the Sufferen farm, I came to the "Slash." This was a glen where a tiny stream crossed the road. When we walked on hot days we stopped and rested there. The Sanctified Church was in that area. As I passed the woods, the Bull Run Mountains came in view. They had caught fire five years previously but the trees now had their full growth and a slight, blue haze hung over them. I would pass Grandma's farm on the right, then cross the Northfork bridge to the railroad tracks. Trying not to walk between the rails, I walked the track until I came to the path that led to the school. The passenger train no longer ran; only a freight went up in the mornings and returned in the evenings.

That scenic walk that I took that fall will forever be etched in my memory. I stayed with Grandma when the weather turned cold. That winter I changed schools and never again walked that same route in autumn.

Mama began to worry that my education was lacking because of my attending a one-room school. She decided to allow me to go to D.C. with Eunice and Harold and stay with my Aunt Geneva. She had Aunt Louise coach me in arithmetic so I would not be behind the D.C. school children. I had finished learning fractions in the fifth grade and was now learning percentages and problem solving to determine which math principle to apply. Imagine my amazement when I went to D.C. and discovered the sixth graders were doing long division.

Eunice enrolled in the ninth grade at Shaw Jr. High and Harold entered Dunbar as an advanced sophomore. I entered sixth grade in Military Road School, a four-room elementary school that went from grades one through eight. It was located in the Brightwood section which at that time was a sparsely populated country area.

Aunt Geneva had nine children when I arrived and in June she had the tenth. Although she lived in a large home, my parents felt my being there would be a burden.

The next school term Mama had arranged for me to stay with her friend, Mrs. Letitia Bagley, who lived in Washington and for whom I was named. I had mixed emotions about leaving my parents; I thought I would enjoy living in the beautiful city home of the Bagleys but was apprehensive about attending a large city school where many children attended.

That fall Mama began teaching at a school near Nokesville. Elizabeth rode to school with her. Papa resigned from teaching and began huckstering full time. The three of us left Virginia to attend the D.C. schools. Eunice had graduated from Shaw Jr. High and enrolled in Dunbar High School. Harold entered his junior year at Dunbar. Mrs. Bagley registered me in the seventh grade at Garnet Patterson Jr. High, a newly-built school. The colored students usually attended old school buildings that had been vacated by whites. She also registered me for private piano lessons from an instructor she knew. This was at Mama's request. Eunice also took piano lessons at the Ninth Street Music Conservatory.

At the time we began our residence in Washington, the city was known to have a tight circle of elite Blacks who formed the

Black Aristocracy. There were certain criteria one had to meet to be accepted in this tight circle.

One, you had to be from one of the old first families, those affluent blacks who had enjoyed freedom for several generations and who resided in D.C.

Two, you had to be of a certain color, although in our generation the color bar had been slightly lifted because some light-skinned women had married darker professionals.

Three, you had to be a long-term homeowner in certain neighborhoods: Le Droit Park, S and T Streets N.W. in blocks from Ninth through Seventeenth Streets, or in some neighborhoods on the "hill," an area from Fairmont Street to La Mont Street.

Four, you had a higher status if you owned property at one of the black resorts, Highland Beach, Colton, or Arundel. You were also accepted if you had friends who owned homes on these properties and who invited you to their resort homes or who rented them from the owners.

Highland Beach was the most prestigious of the three.

Five, one parent or both had to have a college degree from one of the nationally known universities or normal school and be a professional.

Since our family was not well known we were considered to be country outsiders even though we stayed with middle class blacks. The Houston family lived next door to my uncle and we became friendly with them because of our frequent visits to my uncle's home.

Because I was not considered a "Who's Who" daughter I was placed in a section of unmotivated and sometimes disruptive students.

That year was the most miserable year of my life. In addition to being homesick and unhappy in school, I found that Mrs. Bagley was the meanest person with whom I had ever had a close association. Previously my only contacts with women were my loving and doting aunts, my grandmothers and my mother who was also my teacher.

I never called her any name but Mrs. Bagley. She did not physically abuse me but inflicted mental cruelty, always nagging and chastising. She made me wear the same dress to school for three days. I was extremely obedient and a serious student. She was an embittered woman with a caustic tongue. I gleaned some of this bitterness was due to the death of her only child, a son who died in his first year in medical school. Her mother had recently died and I overheard her tell a friend, "I finally learned who my father was. On her deathbed my mother told me he was the President of William and Mary College." I wondered was this the reason for her mean disposition or was it because she was forced to be black?

She was a tall, buxom woman whose skin was so white it appeared doubtful that she had any black blood. Mr. Bagley was a gentle, dark skinned man who held a low-level white collar federal job in the Bureau of Engraving. He never dared to cross his wife.

Their house was new when they bought it five years previously, a rarity in the black neighborhoods. It was a semi-detached, brick designed by the famous black architect, Cassel. Located two blocks from Howard University, it contained four bedrooms on the second floor and a large studio on the third floor. Three Howard University professors roomed and boarded in her house.

There was one pleasant segment of the day that I enjoyed. All the members of the household ate dinner together at the dining table. When we finished dinner at seven o'clock we sat around the table and listened to the radio program of "Amos and Andy." It featured white actors satirizing stereotypical black life with a black dialect, but for some unknown reason it appealed to black people. You could hear every radio tuned to it when you were outdoors. The two young professors would often leave the table and not listen. I now realize they felt the program demeaned black people.

In addition to my suffering under Mrs. Bagley's bad temperament, I had a sewing teacher who was the most contemptible teacher I ever had in my entire education. We were assigned lockers at school and issued combination locks. The combination to open the lock was inside each envelope. I had difficulty working my combination when my seat mate whose locker adjoined mine offered to help me.

My sewing teacher gave us an assignment to buy a pattern for an apron which was to be used in cooking class. The next day I went downtown and purchased my pattern and kept it in my locker. When it was time to attend sewing class my pattern was missing. I received an F and was told to report to her room and stay after school. The next week the same situation occurred when I brought in fabric. Again I received another F and was kept after school causing me to miss my music lesson each time. She accepted no excuses. Frequently she kept the whole class after school for the slightest infraction.

My lunch began missing from my locker. I reported these thefts to my section teacher who replaced my combination lock and I was told not to reveal the combination to anyone. This put an end to the thefts. I was so inexperienced and vulnerable I did not realize my seat mate was the thief.

Our section homeroom was located near the principal's office. One day the principal, an imposing, very fair white-looking lady by the name of Miss Kirkland, came to our room. After glancing over the room she spotted me and beckoned me to follow her to her office. She informed me that she had selected me to be her messenger. She would inform my section teacher that when our bell rang two short rings she was to send me to the office. I felt she selected me because I had light skin.

Near the end of the semester she said, "Susie, when you get your report card, bring it to me." When I received my report card

I was happy to show it to her for I had made the general honor roll receiving all A's and one B in sewing. She immediately took me out of my present section and placed me in the top section that consisted of the children of Washington's black upper class.

My mother knew the matron, Mrs. Watson, a kind, pretty, older woman. She told me to tell her I was her daughter and would she introduce me to girls who could be my friends. She introduced me to two eighth grade girls; one was a commuting student from Maryland; the other was a deformed, hunched-back girl. They both had excellent academic records, receiving straight A's. They were friendly and kind and invited me to eat lunch with them each day. I was not taken in to the elite clique until my senior year.

As there was no phone in Virginia to contact my parents, I had no communication with them until my spring vacation. Papa would stop by Mrs. Bagley's occasionally when he returned from Baltimore after carrying a load of pigs or calves to the stockyards.

Mrs. Bagley usually had a complaint about me. He would leave a note for me and a dollar for my spending money.

He also checked on Eunice at Mrs. Madden's. Eunice said Mrs. Madden would complain to her about Papa's truck being parked in front of her house.

One day Mama and Papa visited me at school. I was ecstatic over their visit.

In October, soon after my arrival at Mrs. Bagley's, we were sitting on her porch when paper boys began yelling "Extra! Extra Paper!" Mrs. Bagley gave me money to buy one. The headlines reported the stock market crash. The news had no significance for me then; later I learned it had brought on the economic depression which affected our family.

That summer I was happy to return to my Virginia home to be with my family. A month before D.C. schools opened, Mrs. Madden visited us and informed my parents she was unable to keep Eunice. My parents knew I was unhappy at Mrs. Bagley's and with Eunice having no place to stay, they decided to move us to Washington.

The economic depression caused my family to suffer economically. Papa's huckstering business had failed which depleted our bank accounts. There were no decent jobs available in Washington. They decided to continue in their teaching jobs and put us in an apartment by ourselves. When I think of conditions in today's world of crime and urban decay, this venture would have little chance of succeeding in these times. The one mistake they made was to send my little six-year-old sister to live with us.

Being the youngest child she had no playmates. With no children for playmates, Elizabeth developed an intense attachment for the adults who cared for her—Aunt Estelle, Grandma Brown and Mama. This hampered her social development. As a toddler she was frightened by crowds and would pitch a tantrum as we entered church. We would take turns taking her outside until church was over.

My mother's cousin, Pete Berry, occupied a one-room apartment in D.C. in the 1700 block of Ninth Street, N.W. There was a vacant apartment on the third floor where he lived. Originally the building was a large, three-story house that had been converted into four apartments. The owner, a young widow, Mrs. Chandler, occupied the first floor. Another couple had an apartment on the same floor with Cousin Pete. On Cousin Pete's recommendation, Mrs. Chandler rented the third floor apartment to us.

The apartment consisted of two bedrooms, a bath, a small kitchen, and a room off the kitchen which served as a combined dining room, living room and an extra bedroom.

Papa moved in some of our bedroom furniture, dining room table and chairs and a couch that opened into a bed.

Cousin Pete promised to look in on us occasionally; otherwise, we were left to ourselves during the week. Each of us accepted a responsibility. Harold cleaned the apartment and fixed our lunches. Eunice cooked breakfast and dinner. It was my duty to take care of Elizabeth—bathe and dress her and take her to school on my way to my school. I picked her up after my school dismissed. Her teacher kept her until I arrived.

The sudden separation from our parents was traumatic for Elizabeth, and the stress of having to adapt to so many changes made her difficult to manage at times. One day she went into hysterics when I brought her to school and I had to return home with her. Mrs. Chandler kept her until we returned from school. She was often sick and caught the measles that year. Mrs. Chandler cared for her during our absence.

Mama and Papa arrived on Friday evenings and left on Sunday evenings. Mama would cook up food to last us two days after she left. As there was no refrigerator we could not save food too long. On Wednesdays and Thursdays we ate hot dogs and canned soup. I would go to a nearby bakery and buy day-old bread for five cents and cake or a package of buns for ten cents. Harold brought a quart of milk which had to last four days.

We had no recreational activity, not even a radio to distract us. After dinner Elizabeth was allowed to go down and play until bedtime with Mrs. Chandler's daughter, who was her age. We would begin studying at that time.

Cousin Pete had a set of encyclopedias that he allowed us to use for reference books and each evening he would leave his morning paper for us to get our news topics for school.

In spite of these hardships, we all excelled in school. Harold had been inducted into the National Honor Society the previous year when he was a junior. Eunice was inducted as a junior that year and I made all A's each report card advisory. Elizabeth also received high grades.

Mama had instilled in us the desire to be as highly educated as circumstances permitted, in order to better our lives. We knew we had a mission to fulfill and nothing deterred us from reaching our goal. We kept our eyes on the prize. What would be the odds in the 1990's of a similar situation to ours occurring? Three teenagers taking on the responsibility of caring for a six-year-old, with no adult supervision, living on a budget below poverty level, no food stamps nor state aid, yet always conducting ourselves properly and excelling academically. At the end of that school year we vacated the apartment and moved our furniture back to Virginia.

Our summer was saddened when we learned Aunt Susie Dick was terminally ill with cancer. I frequently saw her when I visited Helen. She would moan with pain. Dr. Williams came daily to give her a shot of morphine.

Once while I was at her house a severe thunderstorm occurred. She cried out, "I smell flesh burning."

The next day when Uncle Dick surveyed the damage from the storm, he found all three of his horses lying on their backs with their feet up. They had been killed by lightning. Horses stand under a tree in the storm. Lightning had struck the tree and killed them.

That accentuated my fear of thunderstorms.

Papa had a friend who worked at the Y.W.C.A. He was informed by this friend that a new Y.W.C.A. camp had been built in the Highland Beach vicinity. It was named Camp Clarissa Scott. The director was filling the position of cook and maintenance person. Papa and Mama applied for these positions and were hired. They allowed all three of us girls to spend the entire six-week camp season free. Harold worked in a hotel in Saratoga, N.Y.

That was an enjoyable experience. Eunice and I learned to swim and we made friends with the girls of some of the upper class Washington black families.

We received word while at camp that Aunt Susie died. The funeral was over by the time we were able to leave camp. We visited the family the following weekend and Mama brought Helen back to camp with us.

One of the campers was Ruth Smith who was Mrs. Bagley's goddaughter and whom I had met during my stay in Mrs. Bagley's home. Her sister, Hilda Cobb, the wife of Dr. Montegue Cobb, visited the camp and met Mama. Later she wrote Mama offering her the position of caring for her child, Carolyn, while she returned to her teaching job. She indicated that Mama would only serve as Nanny for her child and would not be required to do housework.

The Smiths lived in a large home where six family members lived and all were employed: three were professionals. They were financially able to afford a cook, who was Mr. Smith's mother, and a man hired to clean.

Mama accepted the job although it was almost half the pay she received as a teacher. In the meanwhile, Cousin Pete was instrumental in getting Papa a job in the Maintenance Department at Howard University. The big perk in taking this job was that all of his children would be allowed to attend the University tuition-free. Harold entered Howard University that fall. Mama's prayers had been answered.

The family sold our livestock and moved to a good neighborhood in a three-story, brick house on La Mont Street. It contained two apartments. Cousin Pete had remarried and he and his bride Betty occupied the apartment on the third floor. We occupied the first two floors. They split the rent evenly. Cousin Pete did this as a favor to our family because he too was anxious for us to be educated.

We bought new bedroom and living room furniture and a radio and were able to bring our piano. Enough furniture was left in the Virginia house that enabled us to spend time in summers there.

Our favorite radio program was the Mills Brothers. Papa enjoyed Kate Smith while we enjoyed the crooner, Bing Crosby.
He would buy sheet music of popular songs for us to play.
I became friends with some of the children of elite families
and began being invited to their birthday parties and Halloween
parties. When they first invited me to their homes their mothers
would ask, "Who are your parents?" When I told them, their reply was, "I don't think I know them." Because of my looks and
demeanor they were hospitable to me. Elizabeth had the Miles
children for playmates. They were children of affluent neighbors.

One tragic occurrence marred our happiness that year. One
morning Mama came into our bedroom crying. Harold had
driven to a dance on campus and on the way home a taxi had
struck the car, killing his girlfriend, Dorothy Clark. She was an
only child. When Harold came home his suit was covered with
blood where he had held her taking her to the hospital. The car
was totaled.

That June Eunice graduated from Dunbar. Again we were
proud to see a second family member sit on stage with the honor
students.

The family attended my graduation from Garnet Patterson
and I received honorable mention for perfect attendance. Five
students received honorable mention for having the highest academic standing. I knew I had received better grades than some
of those mentioned and I told Papa so on our way home. The
next day, he went to see Mr. Savoy, the principal, who assigned
a committee of teachers to review my records. They conceded
that I had stood number three in class. The real reason for over-
looking my records was they could not fathom a little country
girl being smarter than some children in upper class families.

Mr. Savoy had the *Washington Tribune,* the black newspaper,
print an item stating that I had stood number three scholastically
in my graduating class and apologizing to my family for the

oversight. This did not make up for the loss of my shining moment I had worked so hard to achieve.

That summer I was in my second year of puberty and began to have bouts of depression. I developed large breasts for my size, a genetic trait that my mother, her sisters and my sister inherited. Mama bought bras for me that did not improve my figure. They were not designed to uplift one's breasts; instead they bound me tightly across my chest which gave me the appearance of having a pillow on my chest. This condition prevented me from running and playing as I did as a child. It was a reminder that my carefree childhood days were over.

My self esteem was further diminished when I realized that I was doomed to be short, five feet one inch, and would not have the lithe, slim body of actresses in the movies that I daydreamed I would have when I became a woman. I was inwardly jealous of Eunice because she was tall and had beautiful, long hair. Elizabeth also had Caucasian hair whereas mine never grew below my shoulders and was extremely curly.

The economic depression continued to grip the country that summer. The World War I veterans had been promised a bonus by the government which had failed to fulfill its obligation. Thousands of veterans marched to Washington to demand their bonus. When they reached the outskirts of the city where they camped, President Hoover sent the National Guard to prevent them from coming into the city.

We had spent August in the country. After Labor Day we returned to D.C., Harold entered his sophomore year at Howard, Eunice entered Howard, Elizabeth returned to Bruce School and I entered Dunbar High School.

Chapter Nine

High School and College Years

The adults in my life told me I could do anything if I was determined and resourceful — I was expected to be ambitious because there was an intrinsic pleasure in excelling.

—Eric V.Copage

Dunbar High School Years

As the school opening date of September, 1932 neared, I had mixed emotions of elation and apprehension. I was thrilled that I would be attending the prestigious Dunbar High School I had heard others speak of so highly most of my life. I had learned much of its history from reading the Dunbar Newspaper *The Observer, Dunbar Handbook,* and Year books that Eunice and Harold brought home. These publications emphasized the high standards of excellence that were maintained and listed names of distinguished alumni who had achieved national prominence.

The greatness of Dunbar was attributed to its exceptional faculty, whose academic credentials compared favorably with those of professors at many United States universities. Founded in 1870 as The Preparatory High School, its first home was the basement of the Fifteenth Street Presbyterian church. From there the school moved to several locations: The Sumner School, Stevens, Myrtilla Miner School and in 1891 moved to a building on M Street between First and New Jersey Avenue, North West.

It was known then as M Street High School. It was at this location that my father was a student. In 1916 the present edifice was
built and named for the black poet, Paul Lawrence Dunbar.
  My friend Jean Brown, who lived two blocks from me, suggested that we ride the street car together on the opening day of
school. When we arrived we met with other students who were
our classmates from Garnet Patterson. Dunbar was also the
feeder school for Shaw, Francis, and Randal Junior Highs. A sign
instructed all new students to report to the auditorium. Boys
were ushered to sit on the right side and girls on the left. This
separation of sexes in assemblies and in section rooms continued
throughout my years at Dunbar. As I sat and waited I read the
poem inscribed on the wall at each end of the stage by the famous poet for whom the school was named:

> Keep A-Pluggin' Away
> Keep a-pluggin' away.
> Perseverance still is king,
> Time its sure reward will bring,
> Work and wait unwearying,
> Keep a-pluggin' away.
>
> Keep a-pluggin' away,
> From the greatest to the least,
> None are from the rule released.
> Be thou, toiler, poet, priest,
> Keep a-pluggin' away.

  After two days of orientation, we were issued Dunbar Hand-
books and assigned to sections. I was assigned to Miss Mary
Cromwell's section along with several of my Garnet Patterson
friends. At the end of the report card advisory, I was one of three
in my section to receive the highest grades. Mr. Walter Smith,
the principal, had a formidable persona. He was bald with
bushy eyebrows. He was an excellent administrator who strove

to continue the traditional high standards of Dunbar. Miss Julia Brooks was the assistant principal and dean of girls, a tall aristocratic lady who took personal interest in the female students. By the time they reached their senior year she knew them all by name. She was extremely diligent in counseling girls on proper conduct around boys. When she chaperoned the school dances she would go to a couple and whisper, "Two inches apart, please," if a couple was dancing too closely. If a student wore a sheer blouse she would send her home and tell her to return appropriately dressed.

Mr. William Saunders was dean of male students; he also taught civics. There were no serious disciplinary problems; some infractions included cutting drill, smoking near the school, being disorderly during study hour, banging on the piano in the armory, or walking the halls without a pass. A student was suspended for disrespect to a teacher. As punishment for breaking school rules, the student was sent to Miss Brooks or Mr. Saunders to sit on a bench outside their offices, and deprived of recess. There was no juvenile delinquency problem. Formal grammar and elocution classes were stressed; everyone who graduated spoke and wrote correct English. The teachers were caring and had high expectations of each student.

At that time, D.C. residents could not vote in any national or local election. Papa and Mama retained their voting privileges in Virginia since they owned property in the state. They both rode to Virginia on election day and voted for Franklin Roosevelt, along with most of the electorate who voted him into office.

The Depression was going into its fourth year and images were depicted in the newspapers and newsreels of the bread lines, men selling apples, the migrant families on the move, and ill clad and ill nourished families evicted from their homes throughout the country. The D.C. residents were not as adversely affected as those in other areas due to stable employment in the Federal Government. District employees were also funded by the Federal Government. In order to equally distribute income of government employees, a law was passed disallowing a husband and wife to receive two government salaries; therefore one spouse (usually the wife) was forced to resign his or her job. This rule affected many black D.C. teachers. Some husbands enrolled in professional schools and entered the professions; others taught in black private colleges, allowing their wives to continue teaching.

Because of the federal salaries that were equal to the white teachers, Dunbar was able to attract the most talented and brightest graduates from the best universities. The faculty remained in their positions with little turn over. Rarely did a senior high teacher take maternity leave; some took sabbatical but were able to return to their same position. This trend helped to preserve the continuity of the Dunbar tradition of excellence.

Those residents who did not have permanent jobs or who had migrated from poor sharecropping farms from the south suffered extreme poverty during the Depression and lived in deplorable conditions in alleys near the Capitol and other areas such as Foggy Bottom. The students attending Dunbar came from middle and upper class homes. Rarely did I get to see the areas where the poorer blacks lived. Occasionally, I observed furniture on the streets where families were evicted.

Roosevelt not only brought Eleanor, he brought men with long histories of caring and public service. He appointed Mrs. Mary Bethune and formed a "Black Cabinet" who advised him on the needs of black people. He put people to work through various federal projects, WPA, and CCC camps. He established food centers where people could get free food.

Papa would never allow his daughters to work as domestics in white people's homes. His reasons, he said, were, "I am afraid some white man might take advantage of your youth and molest you." He worked a part time job in addition to his job at Howard, stoking the furnace at the YWCA at night. Later he was a security guard at Howard for campus events. This was to provide us with a standard of living similar to our peers.

I acquired life long friends at Dunbar during my sophomore year. We were the studious group and attained high grades. Three of us lived on the "Hill" and walked home together in good weather. Another clique was made of pretty, glamorous, light-skinned girls who were popular and usually attracted boys in the upper classes. A few in that group were honor students. School athletic events, football and basketball were not emphasized. Girls did not try out for cheer leaders. Intramural sports took place between the three Senior High Schools, Armstrong, Dunbar and Cardoza, but student attendance was poor at these events.

The main school event was the Colored Washington High School Cadet Corp's Annual Drill Competition between Dunbar, Armstrong, and later Cardoza. It was held in Griffith Stadium and attracted thousands. Male students practiced drilling the entire year for this event. The military instructors were army reserve or retired officers. The cadets wore dark blue uniforms, with white gloves. There were usually three company units at Dunbar. The sophomore students were privates; juniors and seniors had non-commissioned rank and a select group of seniors held commissions in the unit; the highest ranking officer was major. It was the height of every girl's ambition to wear an officer's arm band. This was equivalent to wearing a fraternity pin. The pendant-like band was made of felt in the school colors, red and black. The officer designed it and had it made containing his rank and his girlfriend's initials. It was worn as a small banner pinned at the waist and hung down the skirt.

The mothers who knew each other initiated social clubs to keep their friends' children together. One such club was called "Modest Maidens". I was not chosen as a member but was invited to their parties. The boys who went to Garnet-Patterson formed the "King-Tut-Club". The Shaw graduates formed the "Revelers".

When I returned to Dunbar in my Junior year I had lost weight over the summer. Mama let me cut my hair and have it coifed in a beauty salon. I also wore up lift bras. Mama allowed me to wear makeup. I was ecstatic going to Woolworth's on Fourteenth Street to buy Tangee lipstick and Lady Esther cold cream. Suddenly, I turned from a ugly duckling into an attractive teenager. I had my first date; Morris Murray asked to take me to a party. Papa sternly spoke with him: "Young man, I am permitting you to take my daughter out, but you must bring her home by eleven o'clock. You are to bring her straight home when the party ends." After breaking the ice of my first date, I was asked out by other boys, and late in my junior year I began going steady with Walter Reynolds, a tall blond who looked to be white.

In October of that year Grandpa Nickens died at the age of eighty-two, a man who was the pillar of his community, the bulwark of his family, and beloved and admired by his descendants. He was interred in the graveyard surrounding Little Zion Baptist Church in Greensville, the church that he founded and contributed money for its construction. He planned that this graveyard was to be the burial ground for the Nickens family.

In November Papa and cousin Pete asked the landlord to paint the house inside and make other repairs. He responded by threatening to raise the rent. Rent was costing sixty dollars a month. Mrs. Smith, Mr. Smith's mother who housekept for the Smith and Cobb families, told Mama about an elderly church member and friend named Mrs. Dennis. She owned a luxury type townhouse on Vernon Street, N.W. It was a four storied house in which the owner occupied an apartment on the top floors and was looking for a nice family to rent the first and second floors. She was only asking $40.00 a month rent to the right family. Papa and cousin Pete took advantage of this opportunity and we moved again to 1841 Vernon Street. Our quarters contained two baths, four bedrooms and one kitchen which we had to share. We combined our furniture which enhanced the decor. The Berrys had practically new living room and dining room suites.

Mrs. Smith had filled Mama in on the background of Mrs. Dennis. She had adopted a son who was born out of wedlock to a girl in the South. The father was white. The son became a talented boy preacher. Mrs. Dennis traveled to various churches in different cities where this boy would preach. His performance provided a lucrative source of income. When he became a teenager she sent him to Exeter Preparatory School in Massachusetts and later to Harvard. After he graduated he married a white woman and moved in the best white circles.

Periodically during the time we lived in the Vernon Street house, someone would mention hearing a man come into the house, usually around 2:00 A.M. when our household was asleep, and tiptoe softly upstairs to Mrs. Dennis' apartment. For three or four days we would hear someone typing incessantly; then just as stealthily as he came he would leave at early dawn before we arose. No one ever saw his face, but by his footsteps we knew them to be that of a man. At the beginning of World War II he was pictured in the news and was identified as Lawrence Dennis, a pro-fascist working in a responsible State Department position. He was the author of *Is Capitalism Doomed?* and *The Dynamics of War and Revolution.* Although he had some black blood, he adopted Hitler's racist philosophy.

My English teacher in my junior year was Miss Madeline Hurst. She gave us a long term assignment of writing our autobiographies and suggested we interview our grandparents. After talking to them, I left with a sense of sadness at hearing my Brown grandparents speak of their early years in slavery. On the other hand, I was elated to hear my Grandmother Nickens impress upon me the fact that the Nickens family were always free

Americans. She could go back in our family history only so far. Her parting words were, "Remember now, our people were never slaves." This knowledge piqued my curiosity. How could that be, I thought? The history books said all Negroes were brought to America as slaves on slave ships before the Civil War. My life was too involved and busy through my college years, and later in the role of wife, mother and teacher to pursue this information. Also no one was interested in searching their roots too far in the black race then. Many older people were ashamed of the bastardy spawned by the slave master.

I missed walking from school with my friends on "The Hill". After school I would walk with them as far as Florida Avenue and catch a streetcar home. No colored men were hired to be conductors nor motormen on streetcars during that period. On the car I rode going and coming from school, Mr. William Colvin, one of the Colvins from Virginia who were related to some of our family members, would frequently be the conductor. We knew he was passing and in order not to jeopardize his job we pretended we did not know each other. When I handed him my school car ticket he would squeeze my hand and pretend to take the ticket which he never did. He worked as white but lived as black and continued to work until he retired. At that time, he and his wife moved back to Virginia and lived near their relatives for the balance of their lives. The word "passing" had two connotations for colored people. One spoke of someone passed when they died. When one passed for white it meant he was gone forever from the world of his family and friends. Mr. Colvin was able to live in both worlds.

That year I was the third member of my family to be inducted in the National Honor Society. Near the close of school the part time care taker for Mrs. Dennis quit, and I was asked to take her place. Two weeks later I found her in bed barely breathing. She whispered for me to take a key she kept under her pillow and lock the middle study that contained many books and papers.

We called a woman she had instructed us to contact in any emergency. The woman came, called a doctor to attend her and two days later she was pronounced dead. The rent was due and we did not know whom we should pay. We left without paying and moved back to Virginia for the summer.

Cousin Pete bought a house in Virginia and resigned his job at Howard. He was not totally dependent on his job for income as he was receiving a disability pension from World War I. That summer he was successful in getting the county to provide a school bus to take the colored children to their schools. He was given the position of the school bus driver.

Eunice's date, John Landers, would drive up to see her in his Ford coupe. Sometimes he brought my date, Walter. Papa and Harold did not care too much for John because they thought he was a "show off". He would start blowing his horn a quarter mile down the road to announce his arrival. On two occasions they played practical jokes on him. Once while he was lying in the yard asleep they had killed a long snake. They stretched the snake beside him. One can imagine the startled look on his face when he awoke. Another time they were sitting on the well with a jar between them that contained corn liquor. They were sipping glasses of water and offered John a drink from the jar. Since corn liquor was clear as water they pretended they were also drinking corn liquor. When John took a drink he gulped, gasped and coughed. "How can you drink that stuff?" he asked. Papa said, "It takes a real man to drink this," as he and Harold both finished drinking their water.

The week before school opened we moved to a house on Gresham Place. It was four blocks from Howard. I was entering my senior year at Dunbar, and Eunice was a junior at Howard where Harold was a senior. Harold had become BMOC ("Big Man on Campus"). He was elected to the Student Council, served on the *Hill Top*, the campus paper, and was head of ROTC. Eunice had joined the Alpha Kappa Alpha Sorority, the oldest black sorority, which was founded at Howard in 1908. Lucy Diggs Slowe, the dean of women at the university, was one of the founders and the first dean of women at the University. Dean Slowe instructed the female students in all the proper social amenities. She often had teas and soirees. Eunice was also selected to be in the May Queen's Court, an honor that most co-eds coveted. In her senior year she was elected basilus or president of the AKA Sorority chapter.

Near the end of my senior year I began "going steady" with Charles Brown, a cadet officer and a member of the "Revelers" club. I wore his arm band. My parents attended graduation of three members in the family: Harold from Howard, I from Dunbar, and Elizabeth from Sixth grade. Once again they were proud to see me sit among the honor students on stage.

Prior to Harold's graduation he had received a letter admitting him to Howard University Medical School. The free tuition of the children of Howard University employees only covered undergraduate school. This meant my parents had to pay his medical school tuition.

Virginia had a law that stated any Negro pursuing a graduate course of study that was not available in any Negro College in the state would be eligible to receive tuition money to attend a school elsewhere.

Papa went to his Congressman in Virginia, Representative Howard Smith. Grandma Brown had informed our family that he was her first cousin. His mother and her white father, Mr. Lewis, were sister and brother. Howard Smith had kept abreast of our family's movements without our knowledge. When Papa approached him about receiving aid for his son he was told that Harold was ineligible because he was a resident of the District of Columbia, although they were Virginia residents and taxpayers and voted in Virginia.

He could have bent the rule since Harold was our parents' dependent. He had the reputation of being a racist. I am inclined to believe he knew we were related and resented the kinship; he did not want a colored youth to reach a higher level of achievement than his son.

At a great financial sacrifice my parents were able to send my brother through medical school. Harold worked summer jobs which just covered the cost of his books and clothes. Papa worked extra jobs while Mama continued to care for children. At this time she cared for the daughter of Dr. James Porter, head of the Art Department at Howard University and his wife Dorothy Porter, head of the Moorland section of the Howard library. The Porters lived two doors from our house on Gresham Place.

Living on Gresham Place put me near my friends on the Hill. I became a close friend of a girl named Ann, who lived in a luxury home near my street. Her father was a surgeon and owned a private hospital. She had a weight problem and often talked of committing suicide. We would ignore her threat and always felt she was joking. It was obvious to her friends that her mother favored her sister, often unjustly punishing Ann. Once she told me, "I have decided how I am going to kill myself—by gas because it is clean." I begged her to stop thinking about such an idea. In the summer while we spent our vacations in the country, Ann and other upper class colored girls went to Camp Atwater in Massachusetts or stayed at Highland Beach. When she returned from camp she confided in me that she and her friend Dot had a relationship with two camp counselors who were queer. Another time she told me about a girl at the beach with whom she became friends and who was "funny". (We did not use the word lesbian.) In my innocence, I said, "Ann, maybe they think you are funny." She laughed and asked, "How naive can you be?" Our friendship continued through our high school and college years although we attended different colleges. She attended Howard while I attended Miner Teacher College.

Dr. Monteque Cobb (Dunbar, 1921), the noted anatomist and NAACP executive and Mary Gibson Hundley, a Dunbar teacher, surveyed Dunbar graduates in separate studies. Mrs. Hundley authored the book *The Dunbar Story*. The combined studies recorded the following data listing Dunbar graduates from 1892 to 1954. A third of the graduates finished Ivy League colleges, Seven Sisters colleges and other private, prestigious northern and western colleges.

Those who did not graduate from prestigious white universities graduated from Howard U., Miner Teachers College, Fisk University, Wilberforce, and Lincoln University, Pennsylvania. Eighty-five to ninety-five percent of the graduates completed a college education. Among its distinguished graduates were Charles Houston, first black Harvard law graduate and the architect of the 1954 Supreme Court case regarding school desegregation; Dr. Charles Drew, developer of the blood bank that stores plasma; Judge William Hastie, first black federal judge and first black governor of the Virgin Islands; Howard Fitzhugh, second black vice president of Pepsi Cola Co.; Robert C. Weaver, the first black to be appointed to a Presidential Cabinet position; Edward Brooke, first black U.S. Senator; Wesley Brown, first black to graduate from the U.S. Naval Academy; Elizabeth Catlett, noted artist and sculptor; Sterling Brown, renowned poet; and Frederick Davison, one of the first blacks to attain the rank of Lieutenant General.

My former husband, Charles Brown, received honorable recognition as the first black army pilot. His picture is in the National Aeronautics and Space Museum, a part of the Smithsonian. My sister, Elizabeth Nickens, became the first black director of Social Services at D.C. General Hospital. Our family members are exceedingly proud of having the distinction of being one of only two families to graduate from Dunbar whose entire family were members of the National Honor Society.

In 1954 when schools were desegregated, Dunbar became a neighborhood school and never recaptured the premier status it once held. The old historic building was demolished in 1977. A new inner-city style school building was built nearby. The ties to the former Dunbar High School remain strong. Class reunions are held for those members who are still living and who attended prior to 1954.

College Years

Our parents remained in the Gresham Street house until every family member finished college. It was a semi-detached house with a front porch that extended to the side and was located in a block of low and middle-income homeowners who kept their houses in repair and beautified their small front yards. Our family became friends with most of our neighbors who took an interest in our family.

The nation was still in the Depression and Mama was anxious for us to finish college and get jobs. The only career fields that were open to black women were teachers, social workers, nurses and, occasionally, medical doctors and lawyers.

At that time Howard University did not have an Elementary Education Department. Miner Teachers College was the only black institution that offered training in elementary education. Since there were such few openings for teachers in D.C. on junior high and senior high level, Mama felt it would be best if I attended Miner instead of Howard. She thought I would have a better chance of being appointed in the D.C. elementary fields. Being a part of the D.C. public school system, the tuition was free at Miner. I understood her reasoning. My Aunt Lavinia was against it. She said, "Susie, why don't you send Sue to Howard where she can meet and marry a doctor?" Mama's reply was, "I want my daughters to be independent and not rely on a man for their livelihood."

My years at Miner were uneventful. I took no interest in school activities and would not date any Miner men. Instead I dated several Howard men. I attended all the Howard athletic events and the campus and fraternity dances. I used Eunice's Howard library card to study in the Howard library. Many students thought I attended Howard. Frequently I walked home alone at ten o'clock at night after studying but was never accosted.

The campus dances were held in the Law Library building, while the fraternity dances were held in the Lincoln Colonnade located on U Street under the Lincoln Theater. You entered the dance hall through a long, tunnel-like corridor. It could have been a fire trap with only one side exit. I often think if there had been a fire a large segment of that black, middle-class generation would have perished.

All the big black bands played for the dances. The Lindy Hop was the popular dance which later evolved to the jitterbug. When the band played "Star Dust", several dancers would yell "Our piece!" and rush to dance romantically with their date.

When a big band or a popular singer was billed at the Howard Theater we would attend the matinees on Saturdays and "buck" the show, staying through two performances.

After the movie shows we went to the Hollywood Grill or University Grill on Georgia Avenue for a snack. Prohibition had ended three years prior and I had my first alcoholic drink while in college.

My grades were high enough to allow me to be taken into the AKA sorority. The Howard Chapter sponsored and installed a Beta Lambda Chapter at Miner and I was among the first group of four pledges to be inducted.

Charles transferred from Howard to Lincoln University, Pennsylvania, and I continued to date him when he came in town for holidays and vacations. Whenever he visited to spend the evening in my home, Mama would sit in the dining room with an alarm clock. There was a door between the living room and dining room which she allowed me to leave closed. At ten o'clock she would come in the living room and announce it was time for my company to leave. He accepted her discipline, but I was embarrassed to subject other suitors to spending an evening in our home because of her strict rule. It was puzzling to me why she consented for me to go out on dates but adhered to this strict, demeaning rule at home. I concluded she felt I was more enamored with Charles than any other young men I dated.

When she first met him, she remarked later, "They certainly must not have many lookers at Dunbar." I knew by that remark she implied that he was not the mulatto type of men in our family. I decided then to break that pattern. I was turned off by guys who were obsessed with "good hair". One date blew on my hair to see if I had "blow hair".

I had no problem getting dates in college. Often two or more guys would ask me to dances. I went on walks with them around the McMillan Reservoir located one block from the campus. At times I went to parties at their fraternity houses. Evidently I had the reputation of being willing to smooch but unwilling to go further. On one occasion I was almost date raped; after my tears and pleading with this date he took me home.

My friends were aware of my popularity and now and then asked me to find an escort for them when they were invited to dances. I obliged my sorority sister, Doris Coleman, by asking my brother to escort her to one dance. This date eventually led to a permanent romance and marriage.

I met a Creole from New Orleans who appeared to be Caucasian. His name was Archie Le Cesne and he was attending Howard Law School. He called me a couple of times but I did not encourage a relationship because he was much older. My sister, Eunice, met him later and he asked her for a date.

When she returned home she said to me, "I met that Le Cesne guy who calls you sometimes. He asked me for a date. You don't mind if I go out with him, do you?"

I answered, "No, I am not interested. He is too old for me."

Their date developed into a permanent romance and later marriage.

The summer after my college sophomore year I got a job as a bus girl at Allies Inn, a downtown restaurant. All the waiters and waitresses were white whereas the bus boys and bus girls, cooks, and dishwashers were black. Two Philippine Georgetown Law students were waiters. One became enamored with me and began writing love poems to me. He asked me to go on a date with him. My father absolutely forbade my seeing him again.

He said, "These people are jealous and dangerous."

After one month I quit working.

The summer at the end of my junior year I received an appointment as counselor at Camp Pleasant. This camp was sponsored and funded by the Family Services Association for underprivileged children and some mothers. It was located in Dumfries, Virginia. There were two such camps: Camp Pleasant for colored and Camp Goodwill for whites.

The uniqueness of these camps was that during a week of orientation and training, counselors from both camps ate and slept in the same quarters. If this were known to Virginia authorities, someone or all would have been arrested for breaking the segregation laws.

In 1937 a national hero emerged, Joe Louis, the "Brown Bomber", became the world's heavyweight boxing champion by knocking out Jim Braddock. He was the first black heavy-weight champion to hold this title since Jack Johnson in 1925.

The jubilation the black city residents exhibited was almost as exuberant as when slaves received the news of their freedom. Young, old, light, dark, rich and poor blacks converged on U Street, the black Broadway, to hug, cheer and shout. This scene took place after each Louis victory.

The Rural Electrification Act which was enacted in 1935 provided electricity for our Virginia home. Having electricity enabled us to install indoor plumbing by placing an electric pump in the well which pumped water through underground pipes into the house. A septic tank carried off the waste. This improvement made spending our summers in the country more enjoyable.

Eunice graduated from Howard in 1936. She did a year's graduate work in math at the University. In 1938 she received a teaching appointment in Bates High School in Annapolis, Maryland.

A month before Easter of 1939, Marion Anderson had accepted an invitation from Howard University to perform in concert. Realizing that her performance would draw a huge crowd, the sponsors sought the use of Constitution Hall. The Daughters of the American Revolution (DAR) refused the use of the hall because their bylaws contained a clause that did not allow Negro performers on stage. The Marion Anderson Committee then sought the use of the white Central High School auditorium. The D.C. Board of Education granted permission on a one-time basis. Miss Anderson refused to perform under such degrading circumstances. First Lady Eleanor Roosevelt resigned her DAR membership and Secretary of the Interior Harold Ickes offered the Lincoln Memorial for the concert.

On that chilly Easter Sunday afternoon, my entire family stood together on the Capitol Mall to share this momentous historical event. Secretary Ickes introduced her as having the greatest contralto voice in this century. A crowd of 75,000 stretched in a semi-circle from the Lincoln Memorial to the Washington Monument. There was a thundering applause when this regal lady appeared before the microphone. She wore a bright blue gown covered by a full-length mink coat. A hushed silence ensued as she closed her eyes and began to sing "America." After several classical arias, "Ave Maria" and Negro spirituals, she ended by singing the Negro spiritual "Nobody Knows de Trouble I've Seen," which moved many in the audience to tears. Her exquisite voice lifted the spirits of a whole race to a higher level of thought and hope.

My family attended three graduations in 1939: Elizabeth from Garnet Patterson Junior High, Harold from Howard Medical School and mine from Miner Teacher's College. This was the third Howard University graduation exercises and baccalaureate services where the entire family was present. At the baccalaureate services the president of the University, Dr. Mordicai Johnson, admonished the graduates:

"Do not settle in cities but go down to Brazza's Bottom and uplift your poor, downtrodden race."

I took the teacher's examination that June and ranked fourteen out of one-hundred fifty applicants. Only twelve teachers in my field were appointed that year. I was a substitute teacher until I received a temporary appointment. When I took the exam again the following year in 1940, I stood number five and was the last teacher from the list to receive a permanent appointment that year.

Fig. 1 Paternal Grandfather, James M. Nickens, Sr.

Fig. 2 Paternal Grandmothe Katherine Nickens

Fig. 3 Maternal Grandfather, James Buchanan Brown

Fig. 4 Maternal Grandmother, Irene Barbour Brown

Fig. 5 Father,
James M. Nickens, Jr.

Fig. 6 Mother,
Susie Brown Nickens

Fig. 7 Manassas Industrial School class of 1905. Aunt Louise is second person from left in second row. Grandfather's niece, Lavinia Washington, is first person on left in first row.

Fig. 8 Indian branch of Nickens family—Maly Ellen (Collins) Nickens and James Nickens.

Fig. 9 Mama picking grapes, circa 1913.

Fig.10 [below] Original Tyler home where my great grandmother, Sally Nickens, lived with her sons.

Susie Nickens Ludlow

Fig.11 Delaware school of racially mixed children–Indian, Caucasian and Black–where my mother taught. She is seated in front of door. 1904.

*Fig.*12 Gathering of Nickens family at Ringwood. Mama is first person in second row holding me. Papa is the last person on right in third row; sister, Eunice, is first child on first row; brother, Harold, is last child on first row. Picture taken in 1918.

Fig.13 Original Virginia family house built in 1910.

Fig.14 Great Aunt, Estelle Crawford, with my youngest sister, Elizabeth.

Fig.15 Baby picture of my brother, Harold, 1913.

Fig.16 Manassas Horse Show, 1930.

Chapter Ten

Life in Black Washington, D.C. 1930-1960

*However laudable an ambition to rise may be, the first duty
of an upper class is to serve the lowest classes. The aristocra-
cies of all peoples have been slow in learning this, and perhaps the Negro is no slower than the rest, but his peculiar
situation demands that in his case this lesson be learned
sooner.*

—William E. B. Du Bois,
The Philadelphia Negro, 1899

Washington's Black Elite: The Old Guard

Beginning with the Depression years and up until the period
following World War II, the Washington black upper/middle
class was divided into three categories.

The Old Guard who were fourth and fifth generation Washingtonians and had money, social position and education made
up one category. Most had families of two or three children. It
was considered "not nice" to have too many children. Three
families were an exception: The Ridgely and Jones families who
had six girls and the T. C. Smith family who had five girls. It is
my guess that these families kept trying to have a son.

Due to the restrictive covenants they were unable to buy
new, luxury houses outside the restricted areas. They owned

127

two- and three-storied brick town houses in Le Droit Park and some in other Northwest areas that were well maintained and where they reared their families. They continued to live in these homes most of their lives. The T. C. Smith family owned a mansion on Logan Circle that was originally built by one of the owners of Woodward and Lothrop Store for his mistress. A few other blacks owned mansions on this street including Dr. Fairfax Brown, a Dunbar teacher, and two lawyers, Belford and Marjorie Lawson.

The "Strivers' Section" was a neighborhood between 15th and 18th Streets and R Street and Florida Avenue, N.W. Most of these homes were bought directly from whites. The row houses lining the 1700 block of U Street "meant we had arrived," a journalist, Dutton Ferguson, wrote in the *Opportunity* magazine.

Todd Duncan, who sang the lead in "Porgy and Bess", owned a mansion at the corner of 17th and T Sts. N.W.

Judge Robert and Mary Church Terrell lived in the 1600 block of S Street N.W. Gen. Benjamin O. Davis, Sr. and William Houston, the lawyer known as "Mr. Civil Rights", had residences in the 1700 block of S Street.

In the early 1930's, Dorothy Waring Howard opened Washington's first private preschool for colored children in this block. It was named The Garden of Children School which later included grades one through three. Children of the Negro middle class families attended this school.

Several of my classmate friends frequently invited me to their homes. I was able to observe firsthand their homes and lifestyles. The houses were tastefully furnished and contained several pieces of antique furniture and cherished heirlooms of vases, pieces of silver and china that were displayed on the wooden mantles and built-in corner cabinets. Every house contained a piano whether or not a family member possessed musical ability.

The Old Guard prided themselves on their lineage. Photographs of their parents, grandparents and forbears were displayed in decorative frames and placed on objects throughout the living room and reception hall, on tables, the piano and mantles. All the people framed appeared to be mulattoes or white. The men's faces were exceedingly handsome with black, wavy or straight hair and "keen" features. The women had straight hair, usually in an upsweep coiffure or a large bun on the side. There were pictures of young women with long hair to their waist. All the portraits had serious faces. Many were pictures of family groups. Formal photographs of the present owners were displayed, taken by the local colored photographer, Addison Scurlock.

Their walls usually held an original landscape painting. None had paintings depicting black imagery. A prized group photograph that some families possessed was one taken of a Mother Goose party given by Dr. and Mrs. Burwell where at least forty children of the Washington elite families attended. The children were photographed on the Burwell's spacious lawn. These kinds of children's parties were frequently given by Old Guard parents to ensure the close association and friendships of their children. Gatherings of this type were held prior to the formation of the Jack and Jill Clubs that served the same purpose.

The members of the Negro upper class distinguished themselves by their genteel demeanor, quiet voices, proper attire, correct grammar and gentlemanly conduct. The men wore their coats at dinner in spite of Washington's extremely hot summers. Houses were cooled by electric fans. The women always wore gloves when dressed to leave their houses, white lace or cotton gloves in summer and kid or woolen gloves in cold months. No man would think of entering a house or building without first removing his hat. The men stood when a lady entered the room and always walked on the outside near the street when accompanying a lady. Education was the main passport to enter black society. The women of the Old Guard often married first generation college men who had graduate degrees.

They were conservative and elegantly understated in every aspect. They did not drive flashy cars, dress in the highest fashions or decorate their homes in garish colors. They belonged to churches that had traditional-type worship services. Loud singing, hand clapping and loud emotional preaching were not acceptable. The churches they attended were Metropolitan AME Church located at 1518 M Street N.W. and built in 1886, Berean Baptist Church on Eleventh Street, N.W., Nineteenth Baptist Church, Lincoln Temple Congregational Church, at 1701 11th Street, N.W., Fifteenth Street Presbyterian Church at 15th and R Street, N.W., St. Luke's Episcopal Church at 1514 Fifteenth Street, N.W., and St. Augustine Catholic Church on Fifteenth Street between L and M, N.W.

The most prominent names of Old Guard families were Wormley, Cook, Francis, Cobb, Montgomery, Cromwell, Syphax, Evans, Gregory, Douglass, Terrel, Murdock and McGuire. The daughters from these families, of course, changed last names when they married outside these old families.

The majority of the children attended Dunbar High School and Howard University or Miner Teacher's College. Several were in an economic position to send their sons to Ivy League and other prestigious Northeast and Mid-west colleges. Some of the daughters attended the Seven Sister Schools: Welsley, Smith, Radcliff, Mount Holyoke, Bryn Mawr, Vassar and Sarah Lawrence College.

In summers their children were sent to Camp Atwater in Massachusetts. The boys and girls attended separate sessions. Others sent their children to the Y Camps, the Y.M.C.A. Camp Clarissa Scott at Highland Beach, Maryland.

Many owned resort homes at Highland Beach which they kept exclusive by selling only to those whose backgrounds were compatible with the present owners. By hiring a guard at the entrance road on weekends, they kept the area private and prevented strangers or trespassers from entering the area. The owners gave the guard a list of names of guests they were expecting or who were welcome to visit them. Any unfamiliar persons seen on the beach during the week were questioned as to whom they were visiting.

A few owned homes on Martha's Vineyard in the area of Oak Bluffs.

The husbands in these families were doctors, dentists, lawyers, established ministers, pharmacists, government workers, two undertakers, teachers, and a few who owned successful small businesses. In most cases the wives remained at home and did not work outside the home.

Another category of the black bourgeoise was composed of a younger group of married childless couples consisting of a husband who was a practicing physician or dentist and a few lawyers. They were a generation removed from the Old Guard. Their wives were teachers in the D.C. public school system. Some were couples who both taught in D.C. schools. My cousin had married a teacher and as a couple became a part of this group.

Although they were frequently the offspring of the Old Guard elite and both groups socialized together, their lifestyle was not consistent with that of the old Washington families. They were more or less considered the idle elite who chose not to have children in order to maintain their economic status. If a wife who taught became pregnant, it would be years before she was reinstated in her job. They were economically dependent on two household incomes—the wives' teaching position and the small fees of the male professionals. Members of this group were the victims of the economic Depression years.

Two physicians became moderately wealthy performing abortions. Abortion was illegal at the time; however, these physicians practiced good medicine and were never known to cause a patient's death. Today they would be considered OB-GYN specialists. They also prevented some college coeds from becoming college dropouts. This is not to imply that all childless wives had abortions. Most were diligent in practicing birth control.

Not having the responsibility of rearing children, their main form of recreation was playing cards. They had a propensity for gambling. Women as well as the men, formed social poker and black-jack clubs. Some of the men played tennis on the public courses and bowled in Masonic Temple bowling alley.

This generational group usually lived in two upscale apartment areas, the Howard Manor located near Howard University on Georgia Avenue and an apartment located in "Striver's Section" in the 1700 block of T St. N.W. Some bought and renovated houses in Brookland, a nearby northeast expansion of Le Droit Park. A few bought lots and built new homes in this area.

Travel was limited due to the segregated policy of hotels that barred Negroes as guests. As a result, a network of upper and middle class colored friends and acquaintances was formed throughout the United States. Residents opened their homes to colored travelers upon the recommendation of relatives, friends, members of fraternities, sororities or national social clubs.

"Pearly's Prattle" society column in the colored *Washington Tribune* newspaper often reported which visitor was whose houseguest. She also reported the main social events of Washington's colored society.

Social Clubs began to form chapters in other cities. A chapter of the Boule, the first colored Greek letter fraternity which was originally established in Chicago, formed a chapter in Washington in 1911. The Girl Friend's Club, which began in New York City, formed a D.C. chapter in 1936. The Smart Set originated at Howard University in 1937 and later became The National Smart Set with chapters throughout the country. The Gay

Northeasterners (who later dropped the word Gay), a national women's club, formed a D.C. chapter in 1933. The Guardsmen formed a D.C. chapter in 1938. They were noted for their weekend bashes held in various cities and hosted by the chapter in the visiting city. The wives attended these weekends also.

These clubs served to broaden the contacts of blacks in different cities who had the same interests, education and cultural backgrounds. Attending club and fraternal conclaves established friendships nationally.

Other local clubs were popular in this era. The Mu So Lit Club was a musical, social and literary society that met in a large house at 1327 R St. N.W. The club was exclusively for men.

The Bachelor-Benedict men's club presented debutantes to society at their balls.

The School Club, which was founded in 1907 by school employees and whose members customarily played Whist together, organized themselves into a professional social club. Their continuing goal—the improvement of the quality of education for Negroes in Washington, D.C.

The Oldest Inhabitants Association (colored), which fostered civic pride among its membership of longtime residents, was a prestigious organization.

The Columbian Education Association served as a social service organization

The What Good Are We Club, founded in 1914 by Dr. Frank Jones, was noted for its fancy dress balls.

The fraternities gave their annual balls. The Kappa Alpha Psi gave their Easter Dawn Dance. The Omega Psi Phi, Alpha Phi Alpha, and Sigma fraternities gave formal balls.

Other social activities were musical and literary teas hosted in the homes, bridge luncheons and Highland Beach parties.

In spite of the long history of the Elks Lodge and Free Masons, only a few of the social elite were active members.

Mulatto coloring and hair was the other passport into Washington colored society. This trend originated with the manumitted slave offspring of the white masters. One of the striking characteristics of the free Negro communities was the prominence of the mulatto element. In 1850 three-eighths of the free Negroes in the United States were classified as mulattoes. They were concentrated in Philadelphia, Baltimore and Washington. The mulatto families perpetuated their color by marrying into other mulatto families.

The weddings during this era were on a small scale. Some had formal church weddings with a small reception at home where finger sandwiches, punch and wedding cake were the usual refreshments served. Others had small home weddings followed by a reception at home.

Members of Howard University faculty formed another group of the Negro Washington elite. Most came to Howard from other areas of the United States with cultural backgrounds equal to or above Washington's Old Guard. Their academic pursuits precluded their close association in the narrow circumscribed world of Washington's colored society. Some, however, were members of Washington's old upper class families—Dr. Montague Cobb, Dr. Emmett J. Scott, Sterling Brown, Dr. Kelly Miller and Mercer Cook. Others married members of Washington's colored society during their tenure.

At that time Howard University attracted the most talented and highly educated Negroes in the country to teach in its undergraduate and graduate schools. A few of the most renowned were Ralph Bunche, the first black to receive the Nobel Prize for Peace; Rayford Logan and Carter G. Woodson, black historians; Alain Locke, first black Rhodes Scholar and noted philosopher; Kelly Miller, noted essayist, writer and newspaper columnist; Ernest Just, renowned scientist; and theologian Howard Thurman.

Howard University not only was the seat of learning for blacks, but served as the center of culture for the colored residents. The Drama Department produced plays, and the Music Department sponsored musical concerts featuring nationally famous performing artists. Two Howard professors, James Herring and Alonzo Aden, operated the first black, privately-owned art gallery in the United States collecting and preserving the work of black artists. On Saturday evenings, the Barnett-Aden Gallery became a mingling place for art lovers and artists. The University also held art exhibits featuring the works of Lois Jones and James Porter, two of Howard's art professors.

Members of Howard faculty were instrumental in effecting social change in the nation's Capital.

The male offspring of Washington's Negro upper class families experienced extreme levels of frustration due to the limited career opportunities during the Depression and pre-war years. A few college graduates became police officers, usually directing traffic or serving as foot patrolmen. The post office required a picture with each application. No matter how high one stood on the civil service examination, only those who looked near enough to be mistaken for white received appointments.

Several sons of Washington's upper class were forced to study medicine in spite of having other talents, a situation which contributed to alcoholism. One such person was Frederick Douglas's great-grandson who tragically committed suicide.

As one college graduate put it, "There were no jobs so we kept going to school."

I dare say Washington had the highest number of educated unemployed blacks in the nation during those years.

The most prestigious undertaker establishment was McGuire's, located on Ninth Street between R and S streets. This quote from the Old Guard was often repeated: "One has not been put away properly unless one is put away by McGuire."

An article appeared in the "Pearly's Prattle" social column in
August, 1939 that read:

> Miss Eunice Nickens and Mr. Archibald Le Cesne
> were married in a simple marriage ceremony in St. Jo-
> seph Catholic Church in Alexandria, Va. After a brief
> honeymoon in Harpers Ferry, W. Va., the bride will
> continue to teach in Annapolis while the groom goes
> to New Orleans to work in the law offices of A.P.
> Toureaud, the prominent civil rights lawyer.

The War and Post-War Years

The 1940's began with millions of Americans unemployed
and the tenth year of the Depression. War clouds were hanging
over the heads of Americans caused by Adolph Hitler's invasion
of the European countries. The United States was forming defense units as a measure of preparedness in the event our country went to war.

The War Department encouraged men to enlist by promising
they would be released after one year of military training.
Charles had finished all his requirements for graduation from
Lincoln by February 1941. He enlisted to get his Army service behind him rather than wait to be drafted. As a result of the ensu-
ing events of the bombing of Pearl Harbor and the United States
declaration of war on both fronts, he remained in the Army five
years.

A 366th Infantry unit was being activated at Fort Devens,
Massachusetts, comprised of black men and headed by a D.C.
resident, Colonel West Hamilton. The Howard graduates who
had completed R.O.T.C. were commissioned second lieuten-
ants; a few had higher ranks having served in the Army reserve.
Others joined the 99th Pursuit Squadron being trained at
Tuskegee.

The men were eager to join these units; at least they provided them respectable employment. After war was declared,
"marriage fever" was rampant. The couples who had been

dating rushed into marriages. My friend, Hestelene, married J. Thomas Martin; Jean Brown married Frederick Davidson, who received a regular Army appointment and completed his Army career as a Lt. General.

Charles, who was stationed in Ft. Bragg, N.C., wanted us to marry before he went to Officer Candidate School. I felt I had not experienced life enough and had not allowed myself to have other relationships. I had just begun teaching and for the first time was financially independent. I wrote him a "Dear John" letter breaking our engagement. His mother called frantically informing me that he threatened to go AWOL to see me.

I followed my father's advice and spent a week in Fayetteville, N.C., near his camp, boarding with the Williston family. After meeting and discussing future plans, I agreed to marry him in August.

My friend, Mary (Jones) Freeman, went with me to Baltimore to get the marriage license and I made arrangements with a priest at St. John's Catholic Church to perform our nuptial Mass. Charles secured a weekend pass and we were married in August of 1941. My sister, Eunice, and her husband, Archie, stood with us.

After completing his year as an intern at Freedman's Hospital, Harold accepted an appointment as head of the ROTC unit at Howard University. He married Doris Coleman that September in a small chapel of Howard University's School of Religion. Reverend Howard Thurman performed the ceremony. He was eventually assigned to Fort Bragg. In October their son, James Harold, Jr., was born three weeks before his father was shipped to Liberia with a black medical unit where they were kept for three years treating the native population.

The spring of 1940 brought sadness. Grandpa Brown died at the age of 83. I was saddened because of the hard, laborious life he had, being forcefully separated from his slave mother at the age of five to live among slaves miles away. As a free adult he toiled hard all his life to own and keep his farm and to provide for the education of his children.

He often talked of the Social Security Act that had been passed by Congress in 1935. He hoped it would one day cover farm owners. At the time it became a bill, he was seventy-nine years old. Farmers were not covered until 1950, ten years after his death. After working all his life, he never received a penny from the government. I never remembered him taking time away from his daily farm chores until he spent those few days in the hospital before he died. He was buried in the small family graveyard beneath the large hickory tree on his farm, beside the graves of the two babies.

The fall of 1940 I received my appointment to teach in the D.C. public school system. I was assigned to teach first grade at Walker-Jones Elementary School located at First and K Streets, N.W. and within ten blocks of the Capitol.

The school was nearly one hundred years old. It contained eight classrooms. The twin school, Jones School, was one block away. One principal administered both schools. I was to teach a class on a half-day basis, reporting to school one month at 10:30 a.m. and to begin teaching first graders who reported at 1 o'clock p.m. and stayed until 4:30 p.m., the children receiving only three and one-half hours of instruction. I shared the classroom with another first grade teacher. We changed on alternate months with her teaching her class from 9 a.m. to 12:30 p.m. one month and I teaching the morning session every other month.

I had not been exposed to the seamy side of Washington before. A view from my window looked on the back yards of row houses where people occupied lean-to, tin shacks. They received warmth from an oil bin located outside and heated by fire made from scraps of wood. Many of the children lived in alleys and courts that branched off alleys.

We were required to make a home visit once every six weeks and submit a report of the visit. To my surprise, I was never afraid to venture into these areas to visit the parents. I was always treated respectfully. As I approached, my visit was announced throughout the neighborhood as a way to protect me. Most of these families were recent migrants from the south where they worked and lived as share croppers. The white farmers were experiencing hard economic conditions during the Depression, causing the share croppers to leave the farms. Most of the families were recently from the Carolinas, (which they pronounced "Norse and Souse Calina"). The schools in these poorer areas of the city had become overcrowded due to this mass migration. Some of the men were able to get WPA jobs; some were able to receive relief after a year's residence.

My first grade contained fifty-three pupils. After one month the supervisor reduced the class size to forty-five. Prior to the desegregation of schools, I never had a class of less than forty children. The parents were most cooperative and the children were eager to learn.

They would often say, "If he or she don't behave, jes beat 'em, Miz Brown."

Although they voiced this, they were very caring for their children, sending them to school every day in clean clothes and hair combed. The teachers were required to inspect each child immediately after opening class not only to detect any contagious disease, but also for cleanliness. We inspected for clean hands, clean teeth and ears.

One teacher sent a note home one day telling the mother her son needed a bath. The mother wrote in reply,

"I send him to school for you to teach him not to smell him."

Once when I registered a child her birth certificate listed her first name as Vagina. I asked the mother to pronounce it and she pronounced it the way it was spelled.

"Didn't you mean the child's name to be Virginia?" I asked. "No, ma'am," was the reply. "Who named this child?" I asked.

She answered proudly, "A young white doctor who delivered her in Norse Calina."

I deliberately wrote on the school record, Virginia, to spare her from embarrassment for life.

A teacher at another nearby school told of registering a pair of twins named Gyno and Syph. She was told a white doctor down "souse" named them.

The D.C. public schools were under a dual system. A white superintendent was over all the schools in the city. The schools were divided into two divisions; Division I included all white schools and Division II encompassed the colored schools. Each Division was headed by an associate superintendent who was in charge of the entire Division but directly administered the secondary schools. An assistant superintendent was in charge of the elementary schools in each Division. Dr. Garnet C. Wilkinson was our associate superintendent and A. Kiger Savoy was the assistant superintendent. The staff hierarchy below the superintendents consisted of three divisional directors who supervised a certain number of schools in each division, a principal for each school, and supervisors to assist and supervise teachers. The secondary schools had department heads who supervised teachers and were administered by a principal and assistant principal.

Salaries for beginning teachers were $1,400.00 annually and paid on a ten-month basis. We served one year probation after which we had permanent tenure. The salary increased $100.00 per year for eight years when the maximum salary was reached at $2,200.00. Teaching in the D.C. schools was the highest paying job for blacks during the depressed years. Only low-level federal and city jobs employed Negroes, in spite of their high educational qualifications.

Teachers in the elementary division were expected to spend one-half of their first month's salary buying necessary teaching equipment and decorating their classrooms. I bought furniture for the library corner, supplemental books for the library and a hectograph to reproduce seat work traced from a teacher's copy of workbooks. We were not permitted to allow the children to write in workbooks that accompanied their readers and arithmetic books. This was due to the shortage of funds allocated to the colored schools for books and supplies.

Some principals intentionally withheld workbooks because they appeared to want their teachers to work harder than was necessary. If any pupil lost a book, we were expected to pay for it with our personal money. The children kept the same set of books for at least seven years.

We were instructed to decorate our bulletin boards with pictures from magazines depicting the season, the holidays or pictures relating to the unit of work we were presently teaching. The *Ebony* magazine was not published until 1945; therefore, only pictures depicting white people's activities were available. I would occasionally buy coloring books and paint the faces and arms brown. I encouraged the pupils to color the people in their seat work brown. Even after the publication of *Ebony*, we were advised their magazine pictures were not relevant for the first grade.

We were not encouraged to display the pupils' work as our supervisors felt it detracted from the appearance of the room.

Most of the elementary principals were women who more or less served as task masters rather than inspiring teachers and reinforcing their efforts. Every teacher was required to have a daily plan open on her desk for the principal or supervisor to follow as he or she observed the teacher at work in the classroom. I often wondered if a teacher would be fired if she did not have a written plan for the day.

Not all principals were of this ilk; some were excellent administrators who maintained an efficient staff because they assisted the teachers and practiced good human relations. I was not lucky to have such a principal. My mother-in-law, Berenice

Brown, was an excellent principal beloved by all her teachers. She was principal of the demonstration school.

The most enjoyment I received from teaching was the fulfillment from observing children learn. In the first grade they began the year with no skills and ended the school year proficient in reading, writing and mathematics for their grade level. I did not pass any child to a higher grade unless they had completed a hardback primer and had a grasp of the concepts in math.

Teachers were encouraged to use pedantic speech as good role models for the children. During my early teaching years, children enunciated words clearly at school although they may have reverted to a pattern of speech they heard when they returned home.

I eventually taught in more affluent areas where the children had money for books and field trips. Parents were able to help them at home.

During the war years, schools closed periodically for one day to enable teachers to register residents for their ration books. At various times ration books were issued for meat, sugar, gasoline, heating oil and shoes. In the four years of war, the government stopped the manufacture of every item needed for building military supplies. We were unable to buy new automobiles, radios, appliances, tires or rubber balls. Charles and I had put money down on a new Chevrolet the first of December. When we went to pick it up after Pearl Harbor, we were told the purchase of all new cars was frozen. I was fortunate to buy a 1940 Ford Coupe from a friend who had used it as a demonstrator.

We attended Elizabeth's graduation from Dunbar that June of `41. She missed being salutatorian of the class by one "B." She was the fourth family member to sit on stage with other members of The National Honor Society.

Mama forced her to attend Miner Teacher's College for the same reason she sent me—to insure her of a teacher's appointment. Elizabeth showed her resentment by refusing to take the teacher's examination upon graduation, although she had the highest intelligence level in the family and would have placed high on the list. She took a temporary job teaching in a nursery school that was funded by the federal government as a means of providing day care for children of women who worked in war jobs.

Due to the sudden influx of women taking government war jobs, housing was at a premium for black women. We three sisters and our sister-in-law continued to live on Gresham Place with our parents. The baby "Nicky" as we called him provided much joy for us during the three years he lived with us. Mama stopped caring for other children and came home to care for her own grandchild.

The government built a dormitory, Carver Hall, to house black women who worked in government war jobs. We contributed to the war effort by purchasing war savings bonds, dancing in the colored USO with military men who came into town and making bandages for the Red Cross. Mama and Papa became air raid drill block wardens. When an air raid siren sounded, everyone was ordered to turn off all lights until the "all clear" siren sounded. The wardens checked the block to see that each resident complied with the order.

My brother-in-law, Archie, was drafted into the Army in 1942. He posed an enigma for his white officers. He looked white and had a law degree, which set him apart from most other black enlisted men. Black lawyers were not assigned to the Judge Advocate Generals Corp where the white men received commissions. He was sent to Yale University to study Russian, but the course was dropped after the United States and Russia became allies. He received an honorable discharge in 1944 at the age of 37.

In January of 1943 a friend called me.

"Did you hear that Ann committed suicide?"

A shock ran through me.

"No, what happened?"

"She was found in her apartment with the gas jets turned on. She left two notes, one to her father and one to her mother."

My heart was heavy and I was filled with remorse. Why didn't I tell her father when she so often expressed her desire to commit suicide?

She was a third-year student in Howard Medical School and had married the previous summer.

She had taken me with her to help set up her apartment. It was then she told me she felt marriage would help her to work through some of her mixed feelings about sex. I knew what she meant but would not openly talk to her about her sexuality.

Her buddy, Dot, came to help as we were working.

Dot's mother taught in the same school with me. The day following Ann's death she sent for me to come to her room at lunch time.

"Sue, have you heard any rumor about the relationship between Ann and Dot? She ran out of the house when she heard the news about Ann. I don't know where she is."

"I knew she was Ann's closest friend. Ann intimated that she and Dot had experienced sex with other women," was the only explanation I could offer.

"Now I know why Dot never liked to play with dolls and preferred playing ball with the boys in the street. She is my only child and I will try to accept her as she is. I don't want her to end as Ann." She gazed out of the window as she talked. She told me later Dot returned but was taking Ann's death extremely hard.

I was saddened by Ann's death for some time. "Poor tortured soul!" I would sigh. She knew her mother would never have accepted her relationships with women. She idolized her father and tried to fulfill his dreams of her becoming a doctor and assisting him in his hospital.

Charles received his commission from OCS at Fort Sill, Oklahoma, in 1942 and was assigned to the 351st Field Artillery at Camp Atterbury in Indiana. He returned to Ft. Sill in 1943 for flight training where he received his wings as an Army liaison officer who served as an observer in combat missions. He went overseas in December 1944 where his unit fought in Germany. after the "D" Day invasion.

Eunice was appointed at Armstrong High School in D.C. in 1944 to teach aviation after studying courses in aviation at Catholic University. She took flight training and was issued a student pilot's license.

Roosevelt ran for a fourth term in 1944. Papa had become disillusioned with his presidency. He felt he was becoming a dictator. He also faulted him for keeping the defense units segregated which resulted in Harold's long stay in Africa. He felt he was making poor people too dependent on government by his relief programs. He gave Roosevelt little credit for his Executive Order 8802, knowing he issued it only because A. Phillip Randolph called for 100,000 blacks to march on Washington to protest armed forces and defense industry discrimination. The order banned federal discrimination in these areas. He voted for Wendell Wilkie on election day.

Harold returned home in August 1944 and saw his three-year-old son for the first time since he was three weeks old.

Elizabeth graduated from Miner College in June 1945 and my parents moved back to their beloved Virginia one week later. Their mission was accomplished.

I had rented and furnished an apartment on the third floor of a town house on T Street that was owned by friends. Elizabeth stayed with me until my husband returned from the Army.

Elder Michaux, the flamboyant evangelist, purchased the sprawling 34-acre site that was originally the Benning Race Track and built garden apartments consisting of 595 units. The development was named Mayfair Mansions. The seventeen three-story buildings were considered luxurious for that era. They were completed in 1943 and ready for occupancy for returning black war veterans and their families. Several families of young professionals occupied the units. Eunice and Harold both rented apartments in this complex when our parents vacated the Gresham Place house.

When Charles was released from the Army in 1946 we moved to Mayfair. Elizabeth roomed and boarded with a family on S Street, N.W.

In the spring of 1947 Grandma Brown died. Just prior to her death she was still an energetic little woman; she had cared for seven of her grandchildren from the Webster family after her daughter Mamie had died, and the family's home had burned. Grandma died of pneumonia at a time when the field of medicine had not perfected antibiotics to fight the disease. She was eighty-seven. Although she was active mentally and physically up until the end, I was able to accept her death because I had a new life stirring inside of me. She was buried beside Grandpa under the big hickory tree.

My daughter and only child, Enid, was born June 6 that spring. She fulfilled all my wishes and prayers—beautiful, intelligent and healthy.

Archie took the Chicago bar and began practicing law there. Eunice waited until I had my baby and resigned from the District schools at the close of the term. She moved to Chicago and later taught in the Chicago school system.

Harold opened his private medical practice when he was released from the service and Doris resumed her teaching duties after the birth of their second son, Wayne in 1946.

In April 1948 Grandma Nickens died at the age of 94. She was mentally alert to the end. She had one hundred sixteen direct descendants living at the time of her death. Her funeral was held in a large Baptist Church in Warrenton in order to accommodate all her family which occupied three-fourths of the seats. She remembered every grandchild's name up until she died. She was survived by three great-great-grandchildren.

She kept her family close because she was always fair which resulted in a peaceful family. I never remembered my aunts and uncles having disagreements or being hostile to each other.

She was buried in the family cemetery beside her husband.

Charles re-enlisted in the Army in 1948, first stationed at Fort Dix then at Fort Campbell in Kentucky.

I took a maternity leave from teaching (I later miscarried) and moved with my two-year-old daughter to join my husband on the post. We lived in one of the former barracks that had been converted to apartments. The black officer's club was a barrack which consisted of a jukebox, a bar, a pool table, a ping pong table and a quarter slot machine.

We were forced to exist under the worst living conditions of my life. The converted barracks leaked and were infested with roaches. The black officers and soldiers were prohibited from using the post exchange. We had to shop for our groceries and clothing in the nearby town of Clinton, Tennessee.

On one occasion while shopping in a clothing store, I bought a pair of shoes. I put the shoe box beside me on the counter while I paid the cashier. When I turned to pick up my box containing my shoes, it was missing. I spotted a white woman next to me, holding a shoe box like mine.

I asked politely, "Did you pick up my box containing my shoes by mistake?"

"No," she answered in an ill-natured manner.

I asked, "Would you mind showing me the shoes in the box?"

She refused my request.

I got the manager and explained the situation to him. I showed him my receipt. I requested that he ask her to open the shoe box and show me the shoes. He informed me he could not force her to open the shoe box. I eventually had to buy a second pair of the same shoes that day.

There is no doubt in my mind the manager knew she had picked up my shoes, but he did not want to expose a white woman who might have stolen a colored person's shoes.

The black officers requested a nursery school for their children in our area. We met with a white officer who informed us the cost would be prohibitive to have one in the area. I spoke up and asked, "Why can't our children attend the one on the main post?" His face reddened and he said he would let us know. Later he informed us that we could send our children to the Post nursery school, but we would have to provide our own transportation (the white children were transported in Army busses). I was the only parent who was willing to enroll my child. The other parents said they were afraid their children would be mistreated.

The two white teachers were amazed at Enid's agility, her large vocabulary and her intelligence. She was tested and made the highest score on the IQ test. When school closed she went with me to the cleaners in Clinton, the nearest town. The cleaning clerk said, "You are the little girl whose picture is on the front page of the city newspaper." She showed us the paper and there was a picture of Enid by herself receiving her graduation certificate. She did more to integrate that little southern town and post than any of the black officers who were stationed there.

Four months after I moved to the post, Charles's unit was put on alert and ordered to go to Korea within 72 hours. The quartermaster corps packed our belongings and my daughter and I took the train back to Washington. Charles drove the car to Virginia the next day where I was staying temporarily with my parents and returned to camp the same day by train.

I was reinstated teaching a kindergarten class at Bruce School. Enid was placed in a nursery school. I lived in an in-law's unoccupied apartment until I was able to purchase a permanent house.

His unit fought in the Korean War for two years, returning in the spring of 1952. He wanted to re-enlist, but I issued an ultimatum: "If you continue to serve in the Army, I will end our marriage." I could not abide living under the conditions we were forced to endure and the racism I encountered in the south. I had bought a restored Victorian home in the Brookland area with his permission and completely decorated it to my taste. I also bought my first television.

I was unable to predict the changes that occurred in the armed services after President Truman integrated defense units. Perhaps my attitude toward the Army would have been different if I had been.

He did not re-enlist but began teaching science in the Vocational high school in D.C. He received his M.A. degree from NYU and later became an assistant director.

Elizabeth received her M.A. degree in psychiatric social work from Howard University and worked as a social worker for the juvenile court. She later received an appointment in the social services department of D.C. General Hospital where she became the first black person to be director of the Social Services Department.

I knew three men who were killed on training missions with the 99th Pursuit Squadron. The only man I knew personally who was killed in combat was Theodore Moman. His father was the comptroller at Howard University and had become a friend of my father. He and his wife had visited our Virginia home and were enamored with the peaceful surroundings. He begged Papa to sell him one acre on which to build a home in memory of his son. He stated this was the only spot where he could find peace. Papa sold him an acre facing the pond and the woods with an entrance on Thoroughfare Road in back of our house where he and his wife built a cottage with money he collected from his son's insurance.

Harold and I continued to go to the country in Virginia and most holidays with our families. Elizabeth came during her vacations. Harold bought two acres from Papa that faced the highway and built a vacation cottage. A new, hard-surface road had been built over the old, toll road in 1950. We sent our children to stay with our parents as soon as their school closed. We adults came a week later and spent the entire summer. Eunice and Archie also joined us each summer, driving from Chicago.

Our parents had a water pond dug when they returned to live in the Virginia house. This enhanced the beauty of our house seat. The pond was stocked with blue gills and wide mouth bass. A pier was built at the end. Mama had the pleasure of fishing without leaving our place.

The children swam and fished in the pond. They learned to row a canoe which we named "The Enid" since she was the only female in that generation. Another boy was born to Harold and Doris, their third son, Steven. A tree house was built where the children played. They learned to ride their bikes and practiced driving cars on the country roads when they received their learner's permits. The adults reminisced about family and our childhood and played bridge or adult games nightly. We taught our children to play bridge.

One summer a member of our Nickens family sent us copies of an article by Luther Jackson that appeared in the *Negro History Journal*. The title was, "Free Negroes in Petersburgh, Virginia." Listed in the article were names of several Nickens men who had fought in the Revolutionary War and who were free prior to their service.

We were excited to receive this information. Was one of these men our direct ancestor? We began looking up war records of these veterans, but could not make a connection with our family line at that time.

We all went to the homestead for Thanksgiving of 1952, arriving a day before. Mama informed us Papa was not feeling well and complained of chest pains. He did not eat Thanksgiving dinner with us. Harold wanted to take him back and hospitalize him on Saturday, but he refused to go. On Sunday after we returned to the city, Mama called and said he had a heart attack and died.

We left the children with our in-laws and immediately went to Virginia to help Mama arrange for his funeral. She insisted that he be brought back home from the undertakers where he was laid out in a casket in the living room. He was a full Mason, but she did not want any Masonic rites over him. His funeral was held in the Mt. Pleasant Church in The Settlement where he was a deacon. We did not want the country minister to preach his funeral; instead we had Reverend Holloman from Washington who knew him. The Manassas Industrial School choir sang under the direction of Harry Burleigh, Jr. Papa was the first one among his siblings to die. He was seventy-one years old. He always said he did not want his coffin opened at his funeral so we honored his wish much to the dismay of the people in the community.

Mama insisted that he be buried in Lincoln Cemetery just outside Washington, where most upper class blacks were buried, instead of the family cemetery at Greenville Church. The entire funeral entourage drove 45 miles to the cemetery.

I never experienced extreme grief until his death. I lost weight, cried uncontrollably when I heard Christmas Carols that Christmas and could not bear to have fresh flowers in the house for a year.

I could only take comfort in the fact that he enjoyed seven years of his retirement back at his Virginia homestead, hunting and playing music again with his brothers and playing bid whist almost nightly with his brother, Cook, and two Berry brothers.

After Grandpa Nickens died all the siblings gathered with Grandma to divide the property. He had left 400 acres including the Ringwood farm and four houses that were situated on the property. Each heir received fifty acres, twenty-five on each farm.

Traditionally in Virginia the first born had his choice and usually received more. Uncle Cook took the prime area of the property located near us. Those who had built homes got acreage surrounding their homes. Papa traded some of the Ringwood property with a brother in exchange for acreage on our farm. He had previously purchased additional acreage from an owner whose property adjoined ours which gave him fifty acres plus sixteen acres in Ringwood.

My father died intestate. According to Virginia law in such cases, the widow gets one-third and his heirs inherit the other two-thirds. Harold suggested we sign all our shares over to Mama and let her divide the property among us. We followed his suggestion. Mama divided the property the fairest way she could. Harold bought the sixteen acres of the Ringwood property and gave us an equal share of the money.

He began to acquire more of the property by purchasing from our cousins who had inherited sections. We never considered selling any of our property and were always determined to keep it in the family.

When my mother returned to live in Virginia, she resumed her teaching career and taught long enough to receive her retirement. She had retired when my father died.

Elizabeth lived with her for two years after she was widowed and commuted to her job in D.C. Mama later came to live with me and stayed five years until Enid was old enough to take the bus to her private school.

The developers were beginning to build homes near our property. Manassas was becoming a bedroom community. We were determined to retain our property and keep the country surroundings.

The New Black Bourgeoise

A new, affluent middle class of African Americans emerged in Washington during the post-war period. A large black professional class developed as a result of the ASTP program and the G.I. Bill. A few held high-level government positions.

Our looks and our academic and professional achievements were qualities that my siblings and I possessed which ensured our entre to black society. The proper training in etiquette by my parents and mentors made us comfortable and self assured in any group, white or black.

Several social clubs were formed and noted for giving big balls and social affairs. Among the popular men's clubs were The Hellions who gave an annual Valentine Dance, The Housers for their dinner dances and The Consorts for their New Year's Eve dance. The What Good Are We Club took in several younger members and began having a weekend each year of social activities, including a fancy dress ball and a cocktail party mainly for members and out-of-town guests.

A Washington chapter of the Links was formed in 1948, a prestigious club which originated in Philadelphia in 1946. Its focus was on community service.

The Continentals, a women's community service club, provided funds for shoes for needy school children.

The Jack and Jill Club of America, Inc. formed a D.C. chapter in 1941. It was composed of mothers and their children as a means of the children of the black elite to know and associate with each other. The founding chapter originated in Philadelphia.

The Women, a local social club made up of professional wives, was a status club. The Do-Chi-Kis, a similar status club of which I was a member, formed a D.C. chapter from the original club in Philadelphia. We gave dinner dances periodically.

I was also a member of a popular bridge social club, The Webs, that gave social affairs on occasions.

Harold was a member of the Housers Club. The Houser wives met the same night as the men but at different homes. A big repast was served after which the wives played 25-cent-limit wild poker. The men also played bridge and poker at their dinner meetings. Charles later became a member which automatically made me a member of the Houser Wives Club. Harold's wife Doris joined the Jack and Jill Club.

In 1948 the Supreme Court outlawed racial discrimination in housing, making restrictive covenants illegal.

Affluent black Washingtonians began buying luxury homes and fine old mansions in the northern portion of 16th Street which is locally known as the "Gold Coast." They also purchased homes in Crestwood, an exclusive neighborhood of spacious detached homes on the west side of 16th Street. North Portal Estates was another area occupied by the black nouveau riche and was referred to as the Platinum Coast. Intimate, catered house parties were given in the new luxury homes by the recent occupants. After Eisenhower's order to desegregate all public facilities in 1952, the dances were held in the downtown hotels.

A few socially prominent women made the Green Book, a directory of Washington's most socially prominent women of both races.

Patricia Harris was the first black woman cabinet member and later was appointed ambassador to Luxembourg. Three women physicians had a lucrative practice. Marjorie Lawson was the first black woman to be appointed a D.C. judge.

A late comer to D.C. married a light skinned widowed doctor. She felt her new status would open all the doors to Washington's black society. Her application to become a Links member was rejected. She contacted the National President of Links, Inc., and reported her rejection. The president issued a statement that anyone who wanted to be a Link should be allowed membership. Her justification was that this was a community service organization.

There are now seven Links chapters in the Washington metropolitan area, including three D.C. chapters. The Links, Inc. no longer enjoys the prestige it once had, due to its unlimited membership. The members are to be praised for continuing their philanthropic projects.

During and after World War II, black Washington would boast of at least seven upscale jazz night clubs, including Bengazi, Republic Gardens, Jean's, Crystal Caverns and Zanzibar, all within four blocks. Music was the force that kept the area unique and vital. Pearl Bailey and Billy Eckstein, two local Washington artists, made their first professional appearance at the Crystal Caverns Night Club.

A popular gathering place for the black, upward-mobile society was Billy Simpkin's Restaurant Bar and Grill. Cocktail parties were popular social gatherings where guests crowded around a buffet of finger food and a bartender served drinks. The conversation was trivial chit-chat. We were disenfranchised citizens and were kept out of the political arena; therefore, we did not discuss politics. Instead we told the latest jokes, some risque but subtle (no one used a four-letter word in the presence of ladies). Some today would be considered politically incorrect as they were often ethnic jokes having lower class and ignorant blacks as the butt as well as jokes on whites and other ethnic groups.

We isolated ourselves in our own little world and were only exposed to the plight of the lower class blacks when we taught in the poorer neighborhoods, when the doctors had offices in predominantly black neighborhoods, when the lawyers defended the black criminals or when the social workers dealt with the problems of the poor blacks. After having been deprived of the best things in life, we felt justified in living a lifestyle similar to middle class whites. We assuaged our guilt of frivolity by the clubs making monetary contributions to established charities and black organizations: NAACP, Urban League and United Negro College Fund. At Christmas we took gifts to Old Folks

Home and to the children in Children's Village. Fraternities raised money for college scholarships. The AKA Sorority formed and supported a Health Project in Mississippi.

In 1957 E. Franklin Frazier's book *The Black Bourgeoise* was published. He wrote a stinging indictment about the new class. He wrote:

> The black bourgeoise suffers from 'nothingness' because when Negroes attain middle-class status, their lives lose both content and significance. Lacking cultural roots of the Negro with whom they refuse to identify, they had sloughed off genteel tradition of the small upper class and rejected the culture of the Negro masses.

Integration had come easily to our generation through the efforts and suits of the former generation. We enjoyed all civil rights except the right to vote.

We read about and sympathized with the civil rights struggle that was taking place in the south: the Montgomery bus boycott, closing of schools and the civil rights marches. Only a few Washingtonians joined in the struggles; the Reverend Walter Fauntleroy and a few young ministers joined the marches. Only two black doctors, Stewart Johnson and Dr. French, took time from their practice and joined the marchers.

While Martin Luther King, Jr. was leading the "peaceful resistance" movement against the segregation laws and discrimination practices in the south, a new black activist leader, Malcolm X, was appealing to a large, black lower/middle-class to resist oppression by "any means necessary." The Washington black elite rejected his type of leadership, mainly because of his lack of a college education and his prior criminal and prison record.

With the appointment of two new school superintendents, conditions in the Division II or colored division schools had improved. New buildings replaced the old eight-room schools, supplies were more plentiful, and more colored teachers were appointed which reduced class sizes. The school facilities were more or less equal to Division I when the Supreme Court declared school segregation unlawful in 1954.

The schools were integrated the beginning of the school term without any adverse incidents; however, the white population reacted by a mass exodus from the city to nearby suburbs.

The houses in the Gold Coast area were sold beneath their actual value. In 1959 we sold our Brookland house and bought a house on Blagden Avenue located on the Gold Coast and moved to be near our friends. Teacher's salaries had risen considerably and I was receiving the maximum salary. I had made a large down payment on the Brookland house not using a G.I. housing loan; therefore, we had built a substantial equity when we sold and could afford a more expensive home.

Harold bought a home in Woodridge, an upscale northeast area. Elizabeth moved to a town house in the new Southwest Complex.

Eunice and Archie had become a popular couple in Chicago and were accepted in Chicago's black society. Eunice joined the Chicago Chapter of The Girl Friends and a prestigious women's local social club, The Tri Phis. Archie became a member of a popular men's club, The Druids.

In the middle 50's they moved from the colored Rosenwald apartment complex and bought a spacious condominium in Hyde Park. The one sorrow in their lives was the inability to have children. Eunice had several miscarriages; one premature baby lived ten days.

One may ask why being members of clubs is such an important factor in our lives. In any human society there has always been a pecking order with the elite class on top. We as African Americans have a special need for our closed social sets and clubs. We have needed to bond together as a buffer against white society's indifference and separateness.

The Old Guard in Washington referred to our generation that comprised the new middle class as "New Comers" and conspicuous consumers.

The accomplishments of numerous African Americans in this era instilled racial pride within us. In spite of our steady progress, we still had a long way before becoming a force in mainstream America.

Chapter Eleven

A Divided and Restless City

God gave Noah the rainbow sign,
no more water, the fire next time.

—A slave song recreated from the Bible

The decade following World War II produced a massive rise in the building of large business complexes, shopping malls, and housing developments surrounding the Capital city. Washington had become a megalopolis. The white population in the metropolitan suburbs surpassed the number of whites in the city.

Gentrification of Foggy Bottom and Capitol Hill, that were former ghetto slum areas, caused them to now be occupied by middle-class whites. A large development of apartments, condominiums, and town houses was built in the southwest area. Georgetown had been almost exclusively occupied by whites since the beginning of the war.

These changes pushed the black population into the northeast section, the far southeast, and in the northwest section as far as Rock Creek Park. Large public housing projects were built in the city for the blacks that were being displaced.

The mechanical cotton picker foreshadowed the end of the centuries-old practice of picking cotton by hand. By 1960 mechanical cotton pickers had replaced almost all sharecroppers who labored in the fields picking cotton by hand. This led to a mass migration of African Americans out of the south to the cities of the northeast and mid-northwest. The black population in Washington had increased from thirty percent in 1945 to seventy percent by 1965. The public school population was nearly ninety percent black.

The largest industry in the District of Columbia is the Federal government which could not produce jobs for laborers from the south. Most migrants had few skills that could be used in the industrial business complexes that surrounded the city; also the discrimination by whites confined African Americans to low-paying, unskilled jobs such as janitor or maid or seasonal construction work.

Housing was expensive and in short supply which produced overcrowding in the black neighborhoods. The crowded buildings were neglected by the landlords and public housing projects became rundown and crime-ridden. The lack of decent paying jobs produced more violence and crime.

These were the conditions that existed in most northern cities and in our Capital city when John F. Kennedy was elected president. He was called "The Candidate with a heart" when he ran.

Washington residents were still disenfranchised. The city was run by three commissioners appointed by the President. In 1961 Kennedy appointed our first African-American commissioner, John B. Duncan. He had started in government service as a messenger but had risen to this top level position through the ranks because of his high qualifications and outstanding performance.

Kennedy demonstrated he was sympathetic to African Americans when he helped Dr. Martin Luther King, Jr. win release from jail. In June 1963 he made a televised speech strongly supporting many civil rights goals and sent proposals for several new laws to Congress. He became the black's "great white hope."

During the sixties the country and cities were more divided than at any period in history since the Civil War. Divisions existed in every facet of American society.

We were divided along racial and ethnic lines: black, white, and Hispanics from Puerto-Rico, Mexico, and Central America. Within the African American race, colorism or interracial hostility divided us, light skin versus dark skin. This was present even among middle-class blacks. Those new arrivals to the city felt shut out of the old Washington clique and spoke of that "Dunbar crowd" with disdain.

We were divided culturally and economically. Those who had lived for many years in the ghettoes and housing developments felt estranged from the black middle class, producing "black English" which provided them communication with some cohesiveness but limited communication with the mainstream. They were referred to as being culturally deprived. They felt exploited by the white merchants in their neighborhoods and by the white landlords. There were no job training programs for the migrants and urban poor who lacked skills that paid decent wages and that would allow them to provide for their families; consequently, one-parent families multiplied and forced many to be on the welfare rolls. Many were second and third generation welfare recipients. Teenage pregnancies rose rapidly.

Store-front churches sprang up every few blocks, dividing us in religious worshiping. The middle-class blacks continued to attend services at the old conservative churches.

The disadvantages the urban poor blacks suffered caused many of these families to be dysfunctional; as a result, their children had learning deficiencies, emotional and behavior problems.

College graduates at this time had other career choices than teaching; thus the teachers appointed did not have comparable backgrounds of the early appointees. The teacher's examination was discontinued four years after I was appointed.

These combined circumstances produced the deterioration of the D.C. public schools and lowered the quality of education that previously existed.

I became disillusioned with classroom teaching and began work on my M.A. degree at George Washington University in February of 1962, majoring in educational guidance.

As more middle-class blacks moved out of predominantly black neighborhoods, the distance became greater between the "haves and the have nots." We continued our exclusive social activities. The members of social clubs hosted club meetings in their opulent homes. They took pleasure in exhibiting their hostessing and culinary skills. The clank of gold charm bracelets at the bridge table was a sound symbolizing status. Mink stoles also were status symbols. Elaborate weddings were held with receptions in downtown hotels.

The Circle-Lets, a national women's social club, formed a D.C. chapter in 1963.

In 1960 the Washington chapter of Girl Friends sponsored an annual debutante cotillion. Twenty of the most popular social clubs in D.C. were selected and each club sponsored one debutante. Enid, our daughter, was sponsored by my club, The Do-Chi-Ki Club, in her senior year in high school. We also gave an At Home to present her to our circle of friends. The proceeds from the Cotillion were presented to a different charity selected each year.

Beginning with the 1955 bus boycotts, the turmoil over desegregation intensified throughout the south. Television cameras showed scenes of violence and rage against the civil rights protesters.

The desegregation of Central High in Little Rock had a special significance for me. I was personally acquainted with one of the students, Gloria Ray, who was among the nine students attempting to desegregate the school. I had stayed with her parents in Little Rock on the occasions when I visited my former husband while he was stationed at the nearby army camp, Camp Robinson. Gloria was then a baby in a baby tender. Her father and brother later visited me in Washington.

I watched the abhorrent events take place on television, the hostile mob and the National Guard with guns pointed at these black students to prevent them from entering the school. The National Guard were carrying out the orders of Governor Faubus. President Eisenhower finally took command of the Arkansas National Guard and sent the 101st Airborne Division to enforce the Brown decision.

On June 11, 1963, Medgar Evers, a leading Mississippi civil rights leader, was assassinated. His body was brought to Washington to lie in state at McGuire's Funeral Home. His death brought African Americans together and raised the level of racial consciousness of Washington residents. Many clubs ceased spending money on dances and instead sent money to the Southern Christian Leadership Conference.

•

Washington is always hot in August. On this particular day, August 28, 1963 the heat was oppressive. It was the morning of the March on Washington. The march was organized by A. Phillip Randolph, president of the Brotherhood of Sleeping car Porters, and Bayard Rustin, deputy director of the Southern Christian Leadership Conference (SCLC).

My sister Elizabeth was on emergency stand-by at D.C. General Hospital. Charles was on duty at the Civil Defense Agency. My daughter Enid and I rode the bus down to the Monument grounds where the marchers had assembled. Harold also took his sons to participate in the March. When we arrived the crowd was milling about or eating the food purchased from the vendors' food carts. There was an atmosphere of quiet anticipation. Joan Baez sat on a tall lookout stool with her guitar and sang:

Oh freedom, Oh freedom
Oh freedom over me
And before I'd be a slave
I'd be buried in my grave
And go home to my Lord and be free

A. Phillip Randolph, Rustin, John Lewis, Whitney Young and a white man I did not recognize locked arms and began to form at the head of the line five abreast. Enid and I along with thousands of other marchers of all ethnic groups fell in line behind the leaders. "Let's go!" the leaders shouted and we began marching up Constitution Avenue to the Lincoln Memorial. The event began with several speeches by leaders of the civil rights movement—James Farmer, founder of The Congress of Racial Equality (CORE); a representative of the Student Nonviolent Coordinating Committee (SNCC); A. Phillip Randolph and finally Dr. Martin King, Jr.

During the speeches preceding Dr. King the crowd of approximately 250,000 stood or sat placidly around the Reflection Pool; some took off their shoes and dangled their feet in the Pool. Buses were continuing to arrive bringing bus loads of blacks from the south. Some wore new overalls and red bandanas around their necks to represent the farm laborers. The marchers had come to pressure Congress into passing the civil rights bill and providing more jobs for the poor.

A hushed crowd awaited for Dr. King to begin speaking. He spoke about unity and racial harmony, and each time he spoke the line, "I have a dream," the crowd erupted in cheers. He ended with:

> We will be able to speed up that day when all God's children will be able to join hands and sing in the words of that old Negro spiritual, 'Free at last! Free at last! Thank God Almighty, we are free at last!'

The roar of the crowd's cheering was deafening. Strangers embraced and some cried. I had never felt so emotionally moved.

When the event ended Enid and I went to the Labor Department Building with some friends whose husbands worked for the Agency and stayed until the crowd had thinned enough to allow us to get transportation home. I remained on an emotional high the balance of the evening.

•

Every person old enough to be aware of the enormity of the event can tell you exactly what he or she was doing the moment they heard of President John F. Kennedy's assassination. My school was having a teacher planning day. The children were out of school on that November 22nd day of 1963. The janitor interrupted the teacher's meeting to tell the shocking news. The principal, being insecure and inflexible, gave us a short time to react, then said, "Let's continue."

One teacher spoke up saying, "We cannot go on; our President has been killed. We want to go home and be with our families."

She grudgingly dismissed us. When I arrived home my family was already home.

I watched the drama unfold on TV for the next four days and my tears mingled with millions of other Americans.

After Thanksgiving I took my students on a city tour where we passed the White House draped in black material around the outside of doors, windows and the balcony. Flags flew at half mast on all public buildings. We then visited the grave of Kennedy in Arlington Cemetery and viewed the eternal flame.

When Lyndon Johnson succeeded Kennedy as president, he promised he would work to have the civil rights laws passed as a memorial to his fallen leader. By applying pressure in the Senate, he succeeded, and the Civil Rights Act of 1964 became law.

In 1964, a constitutional amendment gave District residents the right to vote for president. I and most blacks in D.C. voted for Lyndon Johnson for president.

In 1965 President Johnson influenced Congress to pass the Voting Rights Act. He enacted a legislation program called "The Great Society" which included many laws to help poor people. He established the Department of Housing and Urban Development (HUD) and appointed the first black cabinet member, Robert C. Weaver, as Secretary of the Department.

While he was trying to build his "Great Society" he sent large numbers of troops to Vietnam to fight the spread of communism. As the war dragged on, it became unpopular and many demonstrations were held on campuses and around the White House protesting the war. Chants of "Hey, Hey, L.B.J., How many boys did you kill today?" were heard during the demonstrations. They sang "All we are saying is give peace a chance." Another slogan was "Make love, not war," which they demonstrated on the monument grounds with some couples copulating openly.

During this period events were taking place in my own family. I received my M.A. Degree in 1964 and was appointed an elementary school counselor. My daughter, Enid, entered Howard University in 1965.

That year Charles was appointed Assistant Secretary to the Board of Commissioners. Before he was appointed the white Secretary invited us to his home for dinner. He later admitted the purpose of his invitation was to observe our table manners, our ability to converse, and the appropriateness of our attire. One of the duties of the position required that we serve as representatives of the District government at various receptions given for foreign dignitaries who visited the Capital. The Cherry Blossom week was our busiest social schedule.

Our invitations dictated whether I wore a long or short dress. I was required to wear white kid gloves at all events, short gloves for informal affairs and long gloves for formal receptions. Pearl Mesta, the "hostess with the mostest", was always present at these affairs. Being an overweight woman, she usually wore a short-length dress with flat-heeled shoes.

Charles joined the John Carrol Society, a group of influential Catholic men. He was one of four blacks at that time. This group sponsored The Red Mass which was held once a year in February at St. Matthew's Cathedral and dedicated to the country's leaders. The President and members of the Supreme Court attended. We were privileged to attend this Mass and had the opportunity to see in person three presidents: Eisenhower, Kennedy and Johnson. Color television was not available at that time; President Kennedy's hair was much redder than I envisioned. President Lyndon Johnson was taller than he appeared on television.

I received only one invitation to the White House during my D.C. residency. First Lady Patricia Nixon's project was Volunteers of America. Wealthy white ladies, whom we privately referred to as "Lady Bountifuls", would come to the elementary schools and tutor the children. The elementary school counselors consolidated the program. At the end of the school year, each person who participated in the program, which included counselors, was invited to the White House. After all the preliminary security checks I attended the White House reception.

I was impressed with all the pomp and formality. The U.S. Marine Band played in the foyer. Waiters in tuxedos and white gloves served on the White House china and silver service. We were invited to tour parts of the White House that were not opened to the general public tours.

I was deflated when I discovered the cookies were Oreos and some other store-bought cookies. The punch was Hawaiian Punch. Each president is allowed a budget for entertaining. Evidently Nixon was too cheap to allow his wife money for an elegant affair for her project reception.

In 1966 at the end of her freshman college year my daughter married Craig Herndon who also attended Howard. They had a nuptial Mass in Sacred Heart Catholic Church. Afterwards I had a wedding breakfast and reception in our home, inviting sixty guests which included the immediate families and our closest friends.

In late January my first grandchild, Stacey, was born. Since she was the first member of the third generation, my mother and all her descendants went to see her. My brother was a medical officer at the hospital which allowed us to see her the night she was born. When I held her I could see a combination of many family members: light skin from my mother, silky hair from my sisters, grey-green eyes of her mother and maternal grandfather and shortness from her great, great grandmother, me and her paternal grandfather.

More militant black leaders became active. Stokley Carmichael, the newly elected leader of SNCC used a new language of protest, saying "Black Power." He defined Black Power as a call for black people to unite, to recognize their black heritage, and to build their own goals. Other slogans took hold. "Black is Beautiful" and "Say it loud, I'm black and I'm proud."

The young blacks began to accentuate their black identity. They took African names, wore their hair in a bushy Afro style and dressed in African garb wearing the popular dashiki. This type of protest took root among black college students. The Howard University students took over the Administration building and held it for three days until the administration met their demands. After the student takeover, the President of Howard University, James Nabrit, and the Chairman of the law school, resigned. James E. Cheek was installed as the next President of the university. The student demonstration yielded specific concessions from President Cheek.

The young future debutantes rejected the idea of being presented to black society. They voiced their objections to this type of pretentiousness and imitation of a white societal tradition. This resulted in the Girl Friends organization discontinuing the Debutante Cotillion in 1970.

My generation finally accepted being called black as opposed to colored or Negro. We reconciled ourselves to this designation to insure racial unity.

Malcolm X and Dr. Martin Luther King, Jr. continued to be our foremost black leaders. After Malcolm left the Nation of Islam in March, 1964, and made his pilgrimage to Mecca, he significantly altered his world view and racial attitudes. He reached out to major civil rights leaders, especially to the young, militant activists, to work with his newly formed Organization of African American Unity. Just before his death on February 21, 1965, Malcolm went to Alabama to support the voting rights movement. He addressed several thousand Tuskegee Institute students and student activists at a church in Selma, Alabama. He also visited Corretta King while on this southern tour.

An article in the San Francisco Examiner by Clayborne Carson states:

> Malcolm continues to inspire and enlighten black people because we are a society in which large numbers of people experience the American nightmare rather than the American dream. His words remind us how deep and enduring are racial divisions of this nation. They serve as a warning against complacency among those who maintain and tolerate social injustice.

During the late 1960's the Meridian Hill Park became a rallying place for civil rights groups and was unofficially designated Malcolm X Park in honor of the assassinated black nationalist leader.

In the late sixties, Charles and I began having marital problems. On April 4, 1968, I secured a divorce on the grounds of irreconcilable differences. Mary Jones Freeman, my best friend who twenty-six years previously had gone with me to get my marriage license, called me and told me to come to their home for dinner immediately after leaving court. She asked the Martins (Hestelene and Tommy) to come by later and have champagne to celebrate my new status. While we were socializing, Mary's sister, Adelaide Robinson, called and told her to turn on the television. Martin Luther King had been assassinated. That put a damper on our party and I left for home.

The following day when I was returning to my school from lunch, I began to hear several fire engine sirens two blocks away in the vicinity of Fourteenth Street, N.W. I met Stokley Carmichael walking toward the burning area with another black person; as we passed each other I heard Stokley say, "Burn, baby, Burn." This was the beginning of the worst riot in Washington's history.

When I arrived at school the principal received a call from the administration to dismiss school. I rode home in terror; it appeared the entire inner city was on fire. My daughter was home when I arrived. She said, "Mother, Daddy has gone and moved all his belongings; I heard the mob was coming to burn the homes on Blagden Avenue."

This meant her father had taken his gun and left her, the baby, her husband and me with no protection. Thankfully the rioters did not come in our area.

President Johnson had recently appointed a black mayor, Walter Washington, to replace the Commission form of D.C. government. The Mayor with Johnson's approval called out the National Guard. Looting and burning continued for several days. A night curfew was enforced. Only necessary city travel was permitted in the day.

Mayor Washington finally invited the singer James Brown to come and speak on television hoping his appearance and appeal to the rioters would stem the riot. It worked! He told the rioters to stay in their homes and stop destroying their city. The rioting abruptly ceased.

Six months after my divorce I basked in my new freedom status. My friends introduced me to several of their single men friends whom I dated. I sold my Blagden Avenue home and moved into a luxury apartment, Blair House. Enid's family also moved into an apartment.

It was during this 1968 year that we learned that my sister-in-law Doris had a terminal illness, Hodgkin's lymphoma. She retired from teaching and was subjected to a series of treatments for the next seven years.

Robert Kennedy was running as an antiwar and civil rights candidate when he was assassinated in Los Angeles. "Is the slaughter of public figures who speak out to improve the plight of African Americans never to end?" I anguished.

My family sat on the grassy edges of the sidewalk on Pennsylvania Avenue for two hours to await the passing of the entourage that bore Kennedy's body. A special train had begun in New England carrying his body. People lined the railroad tracks from Massachusetts to Washington, D.C. to pay their last respects to an admired hero. When the train stopped at Union Station his body was placed in a hearse and a funeral entourage proceeded down Pennsylvania Avenue past us.

In October of 1969 a peace demonstration against the Vietnam War was held on the Capitol Mall. This was to be the largest assemblage of persons to take place in Washington. One of the leaders of the march was Corretta King who demanded that President Johnson "bring the boys home now." The march formed a nationwide Vietnam Moratorium, a day of reflection and protest over the war. Many African Americans were among the protesters. Black soldiers had disproportionally served in Vietnam.

Three events occurred in 1969 that affected me and my family. My first male descendant and grandson, Robert, was born between Enid's college examinations.

We three sisters had the old Virginia country house razed and buried in a back field. We sent Mama away before its destruction because we felt it would be too painful for her to watch all the memories the house held for her being buried. She stayed in Chicago with Eunice that winter. When she returned a new brick rambler owned jointly by us three sisters was erected on the old house seat.

The third event was my trip to California to attend a professional conference. During my visit, I met my future husband, Paul Ludlow. Our meeting had been arranged by my dear friend, Colonel Thomas Martin. They had been stationed together in Germany and had remained close friends. We were not to marry until four years later.

My family attended the graduation of five members of our immediate family during the years from 1969 through 1972.

1969— J. Harold, Jr. from Howard University Medical School

1970— My son-in-law, Craig Herndon, and my daughter, Enid, received their Bachelor degrees from Howard University. Enid finished cum laude.

1971— Steven, my brother's third son, received his B.A. from Howard U.

1972— Wayne, my brother's second son, received his medical degree from George Washington University. Eric Nickens graduated from Howard University in 1976.

The Civil Rights Movement made tremendous progress possible for African Americans throughout the country. Some D.C. residents broke the color barrier of facilities where they were formerly excluded.

Four golfers, Carl Rowan, columnist and former ambassador to Finland, Charles Ireland, M.D., U. S. District Judge, Aubrey

Robinson, and my brother, Harold, were admitted as members of Indian Spring Country Club in Silver Spring, Maryland.

The *Washington Post* newspaper hired its first black editor, Robert Maynard. General news columnists and photographers were hired including my son-in-law Craig.

Max Robinson became the first black D.C. news anchor man.

Black doctors were appointed to the staff of hospitals where they were previously denied internships and residencies, permitting their patients' admittance.

Gains were evident in the field of law. Five black D.C. lawyers were appointed federal judges. Spattswood Robinson was appointed to the Federal Appeal's Court. Thurgood Marshal became our first African American appointed to the U. S. Supreme Court.

Washington finally achieved home rule. Congress approved the District of Columbia and Governmental Reorganization Act, PL.93-198, on December 24, 1973. The G R Act of 1973 established an elected mayor and a 13-member city council. Walter Washington was the city's first mayor elected by the District. The first city council took office on January 2, 1975. Walter Fauntleroy was elected a non-voting delegate to Congress.

D.C. residents also elected members to serve on the School Board. The first black school superintendent, Hugh Scott, was appointed. My cousin, Norman Nickens, was appointed Associate Superintendent of the Model School System.

Col. Thomas Martin was appointed director of Selective Service for the District of Columbia and Area One Hundred.

During those turbulent years our house in Virginia served as a retreat and refuge from a crumbling city. I would go there on weekends for the peace and serenity that the country-side provided, allowing me to put my life in its proper perspective.

Each summer when we four siblings gathered, we continued to search for our original free ancestors. We spent one day in the Congressional Library searching the ship logs for any person named Nickens who left England during the Colonial era. We found the name of Robert Nickens who left England on a ship bound for Barbados in 1692; however, we never found any record of his arriving in America.

One positive aspect occurred in 1970. I was the recipient of the Agnes and Eugene Meyer Travel Award. This award was made to D. C. teachers for long and outstanding service in the schools. That summer I attended the University of London for two weeks, then visited six other European countries.

While attending the University of London, we stayed in a London University dormitory and ate in the student dining room. I immediately associated the way the food was prepared with Grandma Brown's cooking. They served blood pudding, which I never would eat at Grandma's.

I also heard some of Grandma's oral expressions, such as "water closet" for bathroom. This term originated when English houses did not have running water and a chamber pot was placed in a closet. I also heard the word "necessary" used for toilet, a term she often used. She called the outdoor toilet the "garden house". I thought this was because it was situated in the garden. I learned the English formerly used the same term before indoor plumbing was installed. I drank my tea with milk at Grandma's and in England. She was the only person I knew who called Santa Claus "Kris Kringle" as the English did.

All these English expressions convinced me that her slave master and mistress came originally from England and retained these English customs and expressions. Her mother had acquired their way of speaking.

By establishing residence in Maryland in 1968, I have not participated in the politics of the District of Columbia. Having lived forty years in D.C., I still have an interest and a nostalgic fondness for the City. Returning to my former city twice each year causes me distress to see the crumbling urban areas riddled with crime. Recently, U Street, N.W. is gradually being restored to duplicate the era when it was a thriving center of entertainment and black businesses.

Chapter Twelve

Coping with Segregation and Racism

Racism is pervasive to the point that we take many of its manifestations for granted, believing 'that's life.' Some folks think we can be healed of this disease in a snap, and racism disappears. You can't even shave a little piece off the thing called racism in a day, a weekend or a workshop.

—Gloria Yamato
"Something About the Subject Makes It Hard to Name"
from *Making Face, Making Soul: Haciendo Caras*

In 1921, when I was four years old, I became aware of the gulf between white and colored people in my home state of Virginia. I was sitting in a buggy between my grandfather, James Buchanan Brown, and my grandmother, Irene S. Brown, on the way to the Thoroughfare, VA Post Office. Run by Mrs. Douglass, the postmistress, the post office was a tiny, one-room building beside the road in the Douglass' yard.

When my grandparents stopped for their mail Mrs. Douglass said, "Good morning, Aunt Rena and Uncle Buck," as she handed them their mail.

"Good morning to you, Mrs. Douglass," they replied.

After we had gone a little way down the road I asked, "Is she kin to us?" They answered no.

"Then why did she call you Aunt and Uncle?" I asked.

They explained that she was white and some white people did not like to call colored people Mr. or Mrs. but did call older black people Aunt and Uncle out of respect.

Later I observed when a neighbor woman came to Grandma's to beg for eggs and other food, she, too, called my grandmother "Aunt Rena" while Grandma called her Mrs. Payne. Although the Payne family were very poor white people who lived on a little patch of land behind my grandfather's farm, Mrs. Payne, like Mrs. Douglass, denied my grandmother her title as a married woman.

When the neighboring people came to the farm to cut and thresh wheat, the man who owned and drove the threshing machine was white. Grandma would set the table in the dining room for the colored farm laborers, and the white man would eat separately in the kitchen. "Why are you making him eat in here," I asked. She told me that white people and colored people did not eat together.

On the other hand, my father never accepted the caste system of the South. Once when he went to a store in Haymarket, Virginia, a young white clerk asked, "What will you have, Uncle Mack?"

Scratching his head and pretending to ponder, my father asked, "Which one of my sister's children are you? I don't recall any of my nephews looking like you."

From that time on the clerk called him and my mother Mr. and Mrs.

Once my brother reported to my father that some white children who lived beside the railroad tracks had called him a "nigger." That was the first time I heard that word but I immediately realized it meant something bad.

My father explained to my brother that the poor white people were envious because we had so much more than they. My father constantly built our self-esteem so that we would never feel inferior because we were colored. And we didn't.

The year there was a referendum on the ballot to vote for a bond to build a larger and more modern school for white children, my father drove around the country for weeks urging the colored people to pay their poll taxes and to vote against it. One white man had the nerve to ask my father whether he was going to vote for the referendum. My father said, "No, why should I? My children will not be able to attend that school. I will not vote for such a proposal until you build a comparable school for our colored children." The referendum was voted down. In retaliation, the superintendent of the school district for which my father taught transferred him to a one-room school several miles from home and in a poorer neighborhood. I remember the lecture he gave, impressing upon us the importance of voting against unjust laws.

As I look back and analyze the different reactions toward racism demonstrated by my parents and grandparents, I conclude that my grandparents' subservience was due to their early lives as slaves whereas my father, who was descended from several generations of "free people of color," openly resisted bigotry. Nowadays, he would be considered a black activist.

When we moved to D.C., we found that life in Washington was just as discriminatory. The only facilities not segregated were the street cars. Our teachers made us aware of the injustices imposed on colored people. They gave us assignments to read and write on the inhumane treatment of the slaves, departed from our texts to inform us of the accomplishments of black people and taught us how our race had helped build America. We sang the Negro National Anthem and were admonished to have pride in our race and to behave with the utmost decorum so as not to bring disgrace to it. I remember one poem in particular that Mary Evans, my junior high school English teacher, composed and taught us those long years ago:

This is our flag, this our flag;
For children, don't you know?
The Black man said we'll fight for it;
And thus we'll make it so.
The Black men fought.
Oh how they fought!
And dying this they cried,
The colored child has a country now
For we've bought it with our blood.
So little colored children here
Salute the red, and white, and blue.
Although it belongs to the fairer race,
It too belongs to you.

Although we were barred from patronizing public facilities downtown, our black neighborhood, centered around 14th and U Streets, thrived. We went to the movies on Saturdays to see the serials. The leading black musical stars, comedians and big bands, including Duke Ellington, Ella Fitzgerald, Moms Mabley and many others, came to the famous Howard Theater. Black businesses, including theaters, restaurants, drugstores, and others provided for all our needs.

We were restricted to living in certain areas, but we were a united, caring community. Parents knew each other and each other's children. A watchful eye was kept on everyone in the neighborhood. Homeowners took pride in keeping their properties in good condition. There was little crime. We could walk the streets at night without fear.

Yet, we could not get summer or after school jobs in stores or public facilities or eat in public restaurants. Girls were forced to work as domestics in spite of high school educations. Boys were forced to work as bell boys or waiters in resort hotels away from home. Parents who worked for the U. S. government had the lowest G S (Civil Service) rated jobs although many were college graduates. We could not try on clothes in the better stores downtown. Occasionally if we saw some item that was a good buy we would fake a foreign accent. Using this ruse, we were usually successful in being served.

I remember the civil rights activist Mary Church Terrell leading a picket line in downtown Washington in protest of the policies that prevented us from trying on clothes, eating in stores and being employed as clerks.

When World War II began our black men were assigned to segregated units of the infantry, engineering, transportation, or quartermaster corps under white officers. My brother, who as a physician and a commissioned officer was better educated than most enlisted men, was assigned to Liberia with a unit of other black medical officers. He served three years treating the Liberians because the War Department did not allow black doctors to treat white soldiers and their families.

We wives who visited or lived with our husbands who were stationed in the south had to rent rooms in black neighborhoods and ride in the backs of buses. I always carried my marriage license with me because of an incident in Oklahoma. There, a fair-skinned wife of a black officer was arrested because she was thought to be white and thus illegally married. She was not released until she produced her marriage license which indicated her race.

When my husband received orders to report to the Korean War, I returned to D.C. with my three-year-old daughter. I had the most painful experience of discrimination in my life that snowy Christmas Eve. With no close family around to babysit for me, I had taken my daughter with me to buy a tree and do other holiday errands. When she said she was hungry, I took her into a People's Drug Store intending to buy a sandwich and some milk that she could eat in the car.

But because it was cold and I was afraid she might dirty her snowsuit eating in the car, I sat her on a stool at the counter and ordered her food to eat there. When the clerk handed me a "take out" paper bag containing the sandwich, all my repressed rage at years of injustice suddenly boiled over.

"What is the bag for?" I asked.

"She can't eat in here," the clerk replied.

I threw the bag at her and yelled my outrage, "This child's father is in Korea fighting for your freedom and you will not allow her to eat here where it is warm!"

An old white lady came over to me, patted my arm and said, "My dear, I think this is terrible and we are going to make things better."

I left the store without the food. On the way home, my daughter asked, "Mommy, why did you throw my lunch at the lady?"

"I was angry because she would not let you eat in the store," I answered.

I agonized as to how I could explain segregation to her when she was older and began to ask to eat in the neighborhood restaurants or asked to attend the neighborhood theater.

I was spared the agony by President Eisenhower. He desegregated Washington the day he took office. This was the result of the vanguard of black activists who previously had opposed segregation in D.C. The first place we went to eat was at a Hot Shoppes restaurant. In 1954, when the Supreme Court outlawed public school segregation, my mother cried with joy. "Oh, if only your father were living to see this come to pass," she said. "He fought so hard for better schools for colored." Unfortunately, when the fall term began in 1954, the white people began to flee to the suburbs and when the city integrated most of the black businesses folded.

In 1962, I began earning my Master's Degree at George Washington University in the District. My first class was a Sensitivity Training Course. The class consisted of three middle-aged white men, one middle-aged white woman and me. Our instructor was from the University of California at Berkeley. For the next class session, we were asked to write and share our diaries. The instructor asked me to read mine. I wrote that I was the only black person in the class. When my classmates realized I was black, they showed their discomfort at my revelation and said they thought I was Hispanic or Italian. For the balance of the semester the group discussion revolved around me as a black person. At the end, the woman and two of the men admitted that my presence had some positive effect on their attitudes toward black people. But the other man, a retired naval officer, frankly stated he was still prejudiced against black people and would never invite me to eat at his table.

During my attendance at the University of London in 1970, I experienced an unpleasant and blatant incident of racism. I was the only black in this group of U.S. educators with whom I was traveling. This day we were attending a lecture to prepare us for the school we were to visit, which consisted of children of West Indian parents.

This London University professor warned us that we would see children who act no better than animals, climbing and jumping off places. He held up a book and said, "Your country believes that black people are inferior to whites; it is right here in this Harvard University Report." He continued to rant about their lack of brains.

I was becoming enraged and whispered to my seat mate, "I am walking out."

She whispered, "Stay, maybe you will have a chance to speak."

The lecturer then asked, "How many of you are exposed to these types of students in your schools?"

I jumped to my feet and exclaimed, "I am a counselor in a school of multi-ethnic and multi-racial children. The white students do not test any higher than the black middle class students. Those who have learning and behavior problems are caused by their economic and social deprivation in society. I am a black person and I am sure my I.Q. is no lower than yours."

His face turned as red as a beet. He immediately left the stage, sat in the front row with his back to me, and never uttered another word.

Later, the director of the group, who was a professor at Temple University, commented to me, "You certainly got that guy told off!"

In spite of the disadvantages of being born black in America, living through the Depression, enduring segregation, discrimination and racism and adapting to urban life from a rural childhood, my parents saw their children excel scholastically and go on to have distinguished careers in medicine, education and social work. They instilled in us high family values and sacrificed, struggled and encouraged us to be the best that we could be. As a result we have served as role models for the two generations that followed and who have continued to achieve a high level of success in such professions as medicine, finance and the arts.

I also credit our black teachers who inspired us, held us to lofty standards and took a personal interest in our accomplishments.

I harbor no bitterness nor hate toward any people of a different race. The strong support and love that my parents provided gave me a sense of feeling secure and accepting who and what I am. My teachers taught me to have pride in my race. I have close associations with many white and some Asian persons while maintaining close ties with my family and new and old black friends. I do not accept the label African American as it applies to me because I am proud to be a mixture of white, Native American, and black cultures and races. I am proud to be a descendant of black slaves who became free and black "free people of color" who were always free.

Chapter Thirteen

Church, Religion and Faith

I believe that religious duties consist in doing justice; loving mercy, and endeavoring to make our fellow creatures happy.

—Thomas Paine, *The Age of Reason*

Now I lay me down to sleep,
I pray the Lord my soul to keep.
If I should die before I wake,
I pray the Lord my soul to take.
God bless Mama and Papa and
God bless everybody, and
make me a good little girl.
Amen.

My mother would sit on the bed as she instructed me to kneel, fold my hands and repeat after her this prayer. When she was satisfied that each of us had memorized it, she trusted us to say it each night on our own, which I did faithfully until I reached my teens; then I said the "Lord's Prayer." In reciting this prayer I ascertained my first awareness of the existence of God.

At the age of five when she felt I was able to walk the two miles to the Oakrum Baptist Church in Thoroughfare she sent me to Sunday School with Harold and Eunice. Uncle John, my grandmother's half brother, was the superintendent and his adult daughter, Azalea, was my teacher. We received cards with a picture of Christ depicting a Bible verse. We were taught to memorize a bible verse so we could recite it at the Sunday School picnic. The picnic was held in Uncle John's yard at the close of the Sunday School session. Sunday School began in May after the colored schools closed and ended the end of August.

Uncle John worked as a chef at Fox Croft School, an elite finishing school for white girls. He always served excellent food. As we lined up for him to serve us ice cream, we had to recite a bible verse we had learned. I said, "Suffer little children to come unto me and forbid them not for of such is the kingdom of God."

Now behind me in line was Willie May Ford who was a slow learner and behind her was Russel Harris who never finished the *Baby Ray* primer the seven years he was in school. Willie May had learned the shortest verse, "Jesus wept", which she recited. That was the only one Russel had learned also. All he said was, "He sho did." He got his ice cream nevertheless.

As we walked to Sunday School, we passed the Sanctified Church located in a wooded section by the road. A woman minister who lived in Washington would bring three or four carloads of worshipers from Washington once a month during warm seasons.

Mama warned us never to go in the church. We would hear the feet stomping, clapping and loud singing on our way back from Sunday School. This type of worship was foreign to us causing us to be afraid as we neared the church. We would run fast to quickly pass it.

Sometimes my Grandpa Brown attended these services. My Grandmother showed her disapproval by saying, "He's down there singing and shouting with those darkies." (People of her generation used the term "darky" to designate other Negroes. This was the result of their being house slaves and emulating the term their masters used.)

As I became older I grew to understand why he was drawn to this church; that was the way he worshiped with the slaves as a child in Alabama.

"We would gather in the woods at night away from Ole Massa's house and sing and shout as loud as we wished praising the Lord," he told us when he talked about his boyhood as a slave.

Our minister was not a shouting preacher and the congregation sang traditional hymns. Our families avoided the emotional-type services that were held in some black churches.

My Grandfather Nickens contributed money to have a church built in the Greenville area that was suitable to our family's culture. The Little Zion Baptist Church was built in 1879. Surrounding the church is a fenced cemetery where the Nickens family members are buried.

Each black church in the surrounding areas held church services once a month.

Reverend Mose Strother was the pastor of three churches. He pastored Antioch Church the first Sunday, Oakrum Baptist Church the second Sunday and Mt. Pleasant Church in the Settlement on the fourth Sunday. A tall, portly man with a balding head and ruddy, brown skin, he had a layer of skin that folded on the back of his neck. He always preached wearing a morning suit with a swallowtail black coat, striped grey pants, a black vest and a white shirt with a stiff collar fastened with a black bow tie.

All the country Baptist churches had the same architecture—a vestibule, a sanctuary with rows of wooden pews, and a pulpit containing three massive oak chairs where the ministers sat. The largest chair in the middle was reserved for the Pastor's seat; an assistant pastor sat in one of the other chairs. The windows were usually covered with varicolored paper giving the illusion of stained glass. A large, wood-burning stove was located near the middle. Atop each church was a steeple containing a bell which was rung calling people in to worship and tolled eerily at funerals.

The assistant pastor of the Oakrum Baptist church in Thoroughfare was the Reverend Thornton Johnson, one of the dark-skinned Johnson family who were law-abiding citizens. His father was the founder and first pastor.

The format of the worship service began with the common meter. The minister read a line from the Bible in a sing-song tone and the congregation repeated it in a certain tune. It is thought this rite began when most of the congregation could not read and this method gave them an opportunity to say words of the Bible.

After the assistant pastor said a prayer, Reverend Strother would come to the pulpit, place a handkerchief beside the big bible and read the text on which his sermon was based. As he began his sermon he would pull out his gold watch, look at it and place it back in the fob pocket of his vest. He repeated this in the middle of his sermon and near the end. He sweated profusely and used the handkerchief intermittently to wipe his head and face. I sensed when he was ending his sermons because he would speak quietly and usually end with "Yes, Gawd moves in a mysterious way, His wonders to perform; He plants His foot steps on the sea, and calms the mighty storm."

A hymn would be sung a capella; occasionally Miss Ruth Berry played one of the hymns on the organ she had learned to play with a few mistakes.

Two deacons sat at the front table with a collection basket. The young women often sat in the rear so they could switch down the aisle in their Sunday attire and place a coin in the collection plate. The rest of the congregation would follow. At the end a deacon stood up and said a prayer over the money. The other deacon would announce the amount collected.

The congregation closed services by singing "Bless Be The Tie."

The ministers always pronounced God as "Gawd." They said they were called by "Gawd" to preach. I often wondered how God called them.

The church "Big Meetings" were held in August. We usually attended the one at Double Poplars Church on the first Sunday. There we would see Papa's family and the families that looked like white, the Colvins, Tapscotts, and Grigsbys.

The second Sunday we attended the one at the Thoroughfare church. The families who had moved away to work would return for homecoming. Church was held all day. Between services a big dinner was served to the visiting minister and choir. Mama always prepared a lunch for us to eat in the car. Ice cream and sodas were sold to accompany our lunches.

On the fourth Sunday we attended Papa's church, Mt. Pleasant in the Settlement. Mama made us go inside for the afternoon service because by then some men who had been shooting craps in the woods nearby might become violent after imbibing corn liquor, brandishing a razor or gun and threatening to kill another player accused of cheating.

After my family moved to D.C. we attended Thoroughfare Church during the summers when we returned during our vacations. Eunice formed a choir and played the church organ.

When Reverend Strother died, a Reverend Newman was appointed to the Thoroughfare Church. He lived in Washington and came once a month to preach. He was a bachelor with a high voice and always wore a derby with his morning suit. He later was a neighbor of ours on the street where we lived in D.C. He occupied a house with several homosexual men.

Reverend Garland was appointed pastor of Mt. Pleasant Church. When I learned he had fathered a girl's child and was later fired when he fell down drunk in the pulpit, I became disillusioned with Baptist ministers who were "called to bring the message of Gawd."

I witnessed one baptism in Virginia. When the North Fork Branch became swollen after rains the water was deep enough to immerse a person. Two ministers stood in the water waist-high dressed in black robes. Two deacons stood on the side of the bank to assist the baptism candidates. The young girls with their heads wrapped in a cloth reluctantly went into the water wearing old cotton dresses. When they were dipped the dresses clung tightly to their body curves. The deacons wiped their faces with a towel and assisted them to the side.

Occasionally we attended the Baptist Association meetings where the ministers and church officials from several counties met and argued and politicked to be elected to an important office in the organization.

When I stayed with Mrs. Bagley she sent me to Sunday School at her church, The Lincoln Congregational Temple. She had a neighbor take me and I would join her and Mr. Bagley in church after Sunday School. The church had recently been built the previous year. In comparison to the country churches it was a cathedral. It had a large sanctuary with plush carpeting and a choir loft with an imposing pipe organ in the rear of the pulpit. The church contained Sunday school rooms and a recreation room. I enjoyed the beautiful renditions of the choir and finally understood the content of the pastor's sermon. Many families of the black upper class were members.

We did not attend any church during our residence in the apartment on Ninth Street. One night Papa took Harold, Eunice and me to be baptized by Aunt Geneva's husband who had become a minister and was pastor of the black Baptist church in Brightwood. We were baptized privately in a pool built under the pulpit area.

When we moved to Lamont Street, Mama sent me and my younger sister, Elizabeth, to Berrean Baptist Church to attend Sunday School. Eunice had attended this church when she stayed with Mrs. Madden. This church was formed by a group of Washington's black Aristocrats which included the Francis and Wormley families. They were former members of the Nineteenth Street Baptist Church, but left because too many dark-skinned Negroes attended and the church was not conservative enough for their tastes.

I attended the Howard University Chapel services frequently with Eunice. Harold sang in the choir. At this service I heard some of the most famous black orators who were ministers: Dr. Benjamin Mayes, Dr. Howard Thurman, and occasionally the president of the University, Dr. Mordicai Johnson.

When I became engaged to my former husband, who was a strict Catholic, I began attending Mass at the black Catholic church, St. Augustine, a towering neo-Gothic church in the downtown area at the corner of 15th and V Streets. It is the oldest black Catholic church in the nation's city. A chapel and school were built by emancipated slaves on another location on 15th Street. Later the imposing structure was dedicated in 1876 and named for the African Bishop of Hippo.

Church attendance was predominantly by white Catholics because of its convenient downtown location. Attending Mass in this church was the only opportunity I had to sit by white people in a private building. Their attendance was encouraged because they were financially able to make substantial monetary contributions. As I dropped my quarter in the collection plate, they dropped bills. The irony of this situation was when a black person attended Mass in a white Catholic church, they were relegated to sit in the back pew.

In 1947 the downtown church was demolished to make way for the present Washington Post building. After the city was integrated, St. Augustine merged with St. Paul's, a former white Catholic church built in 1893 whose only black worshipers were the members' chauffeurs who sat in the simple pews in the back of the church. In 1983 the parish was renamed St. Augustine.

About the same time I began attending Mass, Eunice was seriously dating Archie Le Cesne, a Creole Catholic from New Orleans. He began taking her to Mass. We both began taking instructions to become Catholic. My baptism was delayed because I did not agree with the rule prohibiting birth control. I argued with the priest that I thought it was a sin to bring children in this world if one was unable to care for them. I mentioned my aunts having so many children that they could not afford to give them higher education. I was told to practice the rhythm method when I married. Otherwise I would have to abstain from intercourse during the time I was fertile which lasted ten days. I finally conceded to their rule and was baptized Catholic. Hestelene stood with me. Eunice also was baptized and became Catholic.

Papa was somewhat perturbed by our conversion to Catholicism. He felt it divided our family since we no longer worshiped together. It was a sin to attend any non-Catholic Church at that time. Then, too, changes were made in our meals. We could not eat meat on Fridays, nor on Wednesdays and Fridays during Lent. We fasted for twelve hours on Good Friday.

As we left for Mass on Sunday mornings, Papa had the radio tuned to "Wings Over Jordan," a gospel choir that sang beautiful gospel hymns. A feeling of nostalgia would overtake me and I longed to hear beautiful Protestant hymns. The Catholic Mass was recited in Latin as we followed reading our prayer books. The one spiritual uplifting I got was that the atmosphere was conducive to prayer and meditation. I was always a firm believer in prayer although I never knew what Being heard my prayers. I could never pray to the statues of Saints and other figures in the church. We usually attended Low Mass which lasted forty-five minutes. We attended High Mass on Christmas Eve and Easter; then all the pomp and rituals took place with music provided by a choir.

Some Sundays as we walked to Mass by way of Georgia Ave. we would pass by the Temple of Freedom Under God, Church of God. This was a black, storefront church founded and led by Elder Lightfoot Solomon Michaux, a radio evangelist who originated his popular "Happy Am I" radio program. His famous Cross Choir could be heard singing and clapping.

This charismatic evangelist exhibited deep concern for the poor and helpless of Washington. In 1933 the church began the operation of the Happy News Cafe which offered lunches for a penny a plate. Street beggars were put to work selling the church's *Happy News* newspaper in exchange for two meal tickets. Another temple project was the repair of a dilapidated building on the corner of 7th and T Streets to house 40 families who were victims of eviction.

His type of church service was frowned on by the conservative black Washington elite. They attended the churches that traditionally served the upper and middle class black congregations, such as St. Luke Episcopal Church, Fifteenth Street Presbyterian Church, Lincoln Congregational and Berean Baptist Churches.

Eunice and I both were married in the Catholic Church by priests. During the war many mothers and wives attended Novena services held in St. Mary's Catholic Church on Sixth Street, N.W., to pray for the safety of their loved ones who were fighting. This church allowed blacks to attend, but we were segregated and forced to sit in a few seats in the rear that were designated for us. Many times we stood crowded in the rear during services and knelt during part of the services. This was the only D.C. church that offered Novena services.

We reared our daughter in the Catholic Church and sent her to parochial and later to a private Catholic school. She did not perform up to her intellectual level. Feeling intimidated and stifled by the strict and sometimes cruel discipline of the Nuns may have affected her motivation to learn. I conferred with a lay teacher who taught her one year and was told Enid had the second highest I.Q. in the room.

Around 1960 the Catholic Church relaxed many of the rigid laws that prevailed. The Mass was said in English, we were no longer required to eat fish on Fridays, and one could eat before taking communion. You could receive communion without going to confession if you felt you had committed no sin, and you could attend Mass without a head covering.

When my husband and I began to have marriage problems, we received counseling through a Catholic agency. We later divorced and I felt a relief that I no longer had to embrace Catholicism. By then Enid had discontinued attending Mass. She had both of her children baptized Catholic, however. She said, "In case I am wrong."

When I married Paul and moved to California, he indicated that he wanted the two of us to join a church. He had not been connected with a church since he left Coronado to join the Army.

We both joined a small, non-denominational community church where some of our friends attended. The name was The Church By the Side of the Road. Its pastor and founder was Reverend Alexander Jackson, the uncle of Maynard Jackson, the former mayor of Atlanta. This church fulfilled all our spiritual needs. Reverend Jackson represented a father figure who maintained a close relationship with each church member. A talented musician, Phil Reeder, directed the choir that rendered a variety of sacred music: anthems, spirituals and beautiful arrangements of gospel.

Paul and I became very involved and active in the church. Paul was ordained a Pastoral Assistant which was comparable to a deacon, and I taught Sunday School. Three years after we joined, Reverend Jackson retired and died six months later. Over the twenty-one years after his death, three different ministers pastored.

One minister amended the By-laws to the satisfaction of the congregation and was instrumental in converting the church to the Baptist denomination. He had a strong ethnic philosophy and the church services had become the hand clapping, loud singing, emotional type that my family always avoided. Phil Reeder died four years ago. Although the church has many positive aspects such as feeding the destitute, remedial tutoring of students, we find it difficult to sit through the long service where some members become overcome with emotion. I am happy to see the church attract so many young adults. This type of service seems to appeal to them.

During the interim between the last pastor and present pastor, Bishop Roy Nichols was borrowed from his Methodist affiliations and served two years as our pastor. He served on a voluntary basis without any monetary compensation. He uplifted my spiritual feelings and renewed my faith in ministers. His sermons were pragmatic and inspiring. We have a talented organist and music director who has transformed the choir into a superb singing choral group. Our recently appointed minister, Dr. Arthur Scott, appears to be a highly trained and dedicated minister.

I have developed my own religious philosophy. I do not feel the need to belong to any religious sect or church to practice the Bible's teachings of being kind, tolerant and caring to all human beings.

I definitely feel that families should rear children to embrace some type of orthodox religion whether in a church, temple, mosque or synagogue. If children do not have some formal religious training, they search for their own spirituality and can be easily attracted to religious cults. In a structured religious setting they learn moral and social codes of behavior that are acceptable in society; family values are reinforced, and the need to pray to a Higher Being is taught and encouraged.

I still believe in prayer which Paul and I say each evening before eating dinner, expressing our thanks for all our blessings.

I believe there is a higher Force or Being and my faith is renewed each time I see the wonders of nature as I visit the Grand

Canyon or view Yosemite Valley as a gift from the Creator. Each time I hold a newborn baby, I believe.

Every spring and fall I return to our place in Virginia where I was born to walk the fields and bask in all of nature's glory and beauty which I find in this perfect spot on earth. It is then that I think to myself, There must be a God somewhere.

Chapter Fourteen

Life's Changes and Passages

In life, no two things are the same nor do they remain un-changed. Likewise, nothing is always or forever.

Reflections on Life and Love
—James M. Richardson, M.D.

By the end of the 1960's, all of my father's siblings had died with the exception of his younger sister, Katie. She had sold the Ringwood house and built a home near our property where she lived until her death in 1993.

The only living survivors of my mother's family were her sister Louise, her brother Joe and she.

Prior to building the new house, Mama had assumed the matriarchal role. She would begin giving us instructions as we approached the gate to the property of the former house. She planned the meals, assigned us duties, and even told us to go to bed if we stayed up too late. After the new house was built, we reversed roles.

She left all the planning of the new house to us, her daughters. We planned and cooked the meals, hired people to cut the fields, and keep up the landscape. We began to lay out her clothes for her to wear the next day. She allowed us to cut her long hair which had become difficult for her to fix in her usual style.

The family continued to gather in the country during vacations and most holidays. We were all together watching the historical event of the moon landing. When Mama saw Neil Armstrong walk on the moon, she exclaimed, "Just think, I can remember before the airplane was invented and now I have lived to see a man walk on the moon."

The summer of 1972 Paul called from California. "I have just bought a new car and would like you to join me on my vacation. I plan to drive to Mexico or to Canada, whichever you prefer."

"I'll think about it and let you know later," was my response.

I had visited him on two occasions and we had corresponded frequently; however, the distance between us was too great to have a committed relationship.

That weekend I went to the country to spend time with my mother. As we chatted, she suddenly asked, "Sue, whatever happened to the man in California whom you met through Tommy?"

"Funny you should ask me; he just called and invited me to join him on a vacation trip he was planning," I answered.

To my surprise, she said, "Indeed if I were you I would go."

I was astonished; this could not be my mother, I thought, who did not trust me in another room from her while I dated in college. Now she was encouraging me to go off with a man she had never met.

I took her advice and Paul and I traveled to Canada. On this trip he asked me to marry him.

Paul was born and grew up in Coronado, California, an island off of San Diego. His family was the only black family to own property there prior to World War II. He had recently inherited the bulk of the property and had bought out his brother's part. He expressed his desire to sell and buy a home in the Bay Area. Retired from the army and employed by the California Supreme Court, he was financially comfortable.

I promised I would give him an answer after I checked whether I had enough time to retire from the D. C. schools.

When I returned to D.C., I consulted with the retirement section and was informed that with my accumulated leave, I could retire in June.

I called him and said, "Yes, I will marry you. I found out I can retire in June." I let him know I was reluctant to move so far away from my family.

"You can visit your family anytime you wish and stay as long as you like," he promised.

I had a cousin, Fabian Labat, who practiced medicine and lived in Oakland with his wife, Gladys, and two sons. At least, I thought, I would be close to some family.

That year as I was completing my tenure in the school system, I observed the continual breakdown of the families. I had little effect in counseling parents. Most of my duties consisted of referrals to other agencies as the school was unable to solve all the problems of the students.

One day I took a sick child home who lived on a street known to be drug infested. As I parked my car, a woman yelled out the window, "What's this old yellow bitch doing on our street? Kill her! Kill her!" she kept repeating.

I saw several men begin to approach my car. I told the child to run home and I quickly drove away.

How parental attitudes had changed since I began teaching, I thought. When I used to visit parents in the alleys and courts, my visit was announced by a person in the first house, "Teacher coming." Everyone in the area welcomed my visit.

That spring the Poor Peoples Campaign began. After Martin Luther King's death, Ralph Abernathy had headed the SCLC and was the leader of this protest. Tents were erected on the park surrounding the Mall to house over a thousand poor people. The purpose of the campaign was to expose the plight of poor black people and to demand reparations from the government. "Tent City", as it was called, resulted in a dismal failure. Continuous rains caused the grounds to be mired in mud. The D.C. residents rendered some help, sending food, clothing, toilet articles and other necessities. Some beauticians and physicians donated their services to the occupants. I prepared one hundred tuna sandwiches which I took to their food center. The leaders finally called off the campaign and returned the people to their homes leaving the beautiful Capitol park unsightly.

The riot-torn city and evidence of violence becoming more prevalent convinced me it was to my advantage to leave Washington. I welcomed the change and a new life in California with Paul.

Harold and Doris met Paul when they stopped in San Francisco on a trip to Hawaii. When he returned home, he said he was favorably impressed with Paul. He was impressed by his gentlemanly demeanor and his lifestyle. Paul is an avid and excellent golfer.

Mama smiled as she remarked, "I knew I could depend on Tommy Martin to do the right thing for Sue."

Enid and her husband had permanent positions and were financially independent. Enid was appointed psychometrist in the D.C. schools; Craig was assigned as a news photographer at the *Washington Post*. She later became assistant to the D.C. Mayor. She is presently employed as a program director at the Department of Education.

My sister, Elizabeth, was diagnosed as an insulin-dependent diabetic while in her twenties. The stress from her job exacerbated her diabetic condition. She retired on disability the same month as I. She and Mama moved to the Virginia house where they established their permanent residence.

The first years of her retirement were spent pursuing the history of our families. Later she was the first black to be appointed to the Prince William Welfare Board. She eventually became involved in Virginia politics and served on several commissions of

Prince William County which did not allow her time to continue and complete the search of our family roots.

Paul had selected a house situated on the border of Berkeley and Oakland in the predominately white area of Rockridge. The owner honored his request that he not hold "open house" until I arrived two weeks later and have a chance to see it. I arrived in April and toured the house. I liked all its features and surroundings immediately. That evening Paul placed a deposit and a settlement date was set for May.

We were married in a ceremony in Las Vegas two days after my arrival. Two weeks later the Labats gave a reception for us in their home. At this time I was introduced to a large segment of the Bay Area black society. To my delight, three of the guest couples attending were people I had known in D.C., who had moved to the Bay Area; Harry and Zenobia Payne had been my neighbors on Gresham Place. Lucy and Tommy Andrews were former Dunbar alumni. I had known Lucy since junior high. Tommy was now practicing dentistry in the area. Charlotte Ridgely Lewis and her husband, Burton Lewis, greeted us and welcomed me. Charlotte practiced law and Burton was director of a training center.

I received a warm welcome to California. Some of the people I met at the reception formed a bridge club for my benefit. I was later taken into another bridge club composed of professional men's wives.

Paul returned to Washington with me in June at which time he met my family and friends. I signed my retirement papers and after attending a round of "good-by" parties we moved into our California home.

The former white owner seemed extremely anxious for us to buy the house, making many concessions that we requested. I began to think there was something wrong with the house. Paul rejected my idea that we get a contractor to inspect the house.

The owner had given us the original plans describing all the materials. It was a solidly-built house.

I moved my furniture and completely decorated our new home to my taste.

The white neighbors on both sides were cordial and friendly. The older couple whose property adjoined our driveway avoided speaking to us. One neighbor informed us our former owner had a running feud with these neighbors. Now I realized why he was anxious to sell his house to us. He wanted to spite his feuding neighbors by selling to blacks. These neighbors moved by Christmas. I had a pre-conceived notion that I was moving to liberal California; instead, I experienced this racism soon after my arrival. I must admit this incident was my only racist experience as a California resident.

I quickly adjusted to my new life. Paul proved to be a devoted and caring husband. I became active in my community, serving six years on the Oakland Museum Board of Directors and chairing the Black Film Makers Hall of Fame Gala. We both became active in a church we joined.

Gladys Labat served as my surrogate sister. We exchanged holiday dinners which diminished some of my nostalgia to be with my family at Christmas and Thanksgiving.

I renewed my friendship with Wene Watson and her husband, Dr. James Watson, who formerly lived in Washington and now lived in Oakland. Wene and I were members of the Web's Club in D.C. I also taught her two older children. She, Gladys and I organized a San Francisco Chapter of the National Smart Set. Sadly Gladys died after a brief illness the day the National Chapter admitted our group as a chapter.

When I met and became more involved with the people in the Bay Area, I immediately became aware of the color variations of the upper class blacks. No longer did I attend social functions where everyone had light skin as opposed to the social gatherings I attended in D.C.

With a few exceptions, the professional men—doctors, lawyers, judges and successful business men—were handsome brown men. A few of the Howard University alumni had lighter complexions. I observed most of the men married women of a lighter hue. As I grew to know and become friends with these men I find they are more sincere, more professionally dedicated, and more committed to charitable causes than their D.C. counterparts. They do not give elaborate affairs just to impress each other. Most of the social affairs are fund raisers for black charities.

The men are self-assured and self-actualized.

My attendance at a Links' Debutante Ball was an eye-opener. The debs ranged in color with a large percentage having dark brown skin. How wonderful, I thought, that these girls were selected to be presented to black society. They were beautiful in their white formal gowns, walking regally down the aisle on their fathers' arms and bowing gracefully on stage. I could not help but compare them to the light-complexioned debutantes at the D.C. Chapter of Girl Friends debutante balls.

I realized I had lost my color bias and my rejection of Afrocentric culture when I began enjoying the gospel renditions of the church choir.

On each visit to my former city, I am conscious of the erosion of the color line. The two light-skinned Howard University presidents, Dr. Mordicai Johnson and James Nabrit, have been replaced with brown-skinned Dr. Cheek, who has been succeeded by other dark-skinned presidents. The Howard University student body ranges in a spectrum of various shades of tan and brown.

Elected congressional leaders are an array of skin color, from ivory to dark brown, unlike their predecessors, Oscar De Priest, Adam Clayton Powell, and Edward Brooke. Much to many people's chagrin, Clarence Thomas has replaced Thurgood Marshal as Supreme Court Justice. The objection is not to his color, but his conservative philosophy. Dark-skinned Marion Barry has been elected D.C. mayor three times.

Black movie actors and actresses are featured regularly in starring roles. The dark-skinned male stars appear to get more starring roles than light-skinned males.

Beautiful black models are appearing in magazines. Several African American women participate in the Miss America Beauty Pageant. Two were elected beauty queens. Brown-skinned Oprah Winfrey has become the richest and most popular talk show hostess. Dark skinned, handsome Vernon Jordon is one of the most powerful men in the country.

These darker celebrities should serve as role models for dark-skinned young people in realizing their dreams.

On one of my visits to Virginia to see my family, a cousin's widow had brought over a small boy she had adopted. The next day my mother commented, "That certainly was an ugly little boy she adopted."

For the first time in my life I raised my voice in anger to my mother. "Mama, you have been making unkind remarks about people all my life. That was not an ugly little boy. He was well-behaved. You only called him ugly because he was dark!"

She was in her nineties at the time and I knew her attitude would never change. I knew she did not have a dislike for dark colored people because I remembered how she cared for her pupils. She was reared in an era when mulattoes advanced further, both educationally and occupationally, than blacks who were dark skinned. She only wanted the best opportunities for her children and knew our light skin would give us a better chance in achieving a higher education and gaining social status than if we had been dark.

My brother Harold never regained his self esteem after Grandma Kate's remark about his blackness. Both of his wives appeared to be Caucasian. He said he wanted to be certain his children were light-skinned with straight hair when he married Doris.

Paul belongs to a national black golfer's group that meets every Labor Day weekend at various posh resorts to play in a tournament they call "The Ghetto Open." Some of the wives objected to the name, thinking the hotels may fail to book us under that title. The men emphatically insist on this tournament name, saying they want the white people to see how far they have come from the ghetto. As yet they have never been rejected.

I have a close relationship with a friend, Marie Calloway, who is a nationally known black artist. Although she is light-skinned, she has a strong Afrocentric philosophy. Through her influence I have learned to appreciate works of black artists, black authors and black imagery.

Color discrimination is deeply rooted in our nation's history. These prejudices persist among African Americans today. Alvin F. Poussant, M.D., states "It illustrates how deeply racism continues to intrude on the black psyche and behavior." The members of the elite national social clubs continue to be predominantly light-skinned. This may be due to their eastern origins. The newer chapters, however, do have several attractive darker-skinned members, who have attained a high professional status and are successful in businesses. Some are judges; others hold executive positions. The by-laws of the National Smart Set require that each group applying for membership send a picture prior to being voted in. I plan to question the national officers as to the purpose of requiring a picture before being admitted.

The Nickens women no longer need to depend on the white man's generosity and bear his children as their female ancestors were wont to do. The Brown women no longer serve as breeders for their white masters as our former slave ancestors were forced to do. Consequently, the descendants three generations later had fewer white racial characteristics.

At a recent Nickens-Colvin reunion, a family member said in jest, "Those old folks up in the graveyard must be spinning in their graves if they are looking down on some of their descendants today." I have coined a term for this transition as "The browning of the Nickens families." The trend of racial intermarriage will undoubtedly produce more mulattoes.

The Baby Boomer generation benefitted by the affirmative action programs which gave African Americans the long-denied opportunity to become entrenched as corporate executives, captains of industry, white collar professionals, chief executives of cities, and federal lawmakers. At the same time, we see blacks trapped in low-paying jobs in less affluent communities.

Paul kept his promise concerning my visits with my family. I have returned to Washington and Virginia twice each year, usually in the fall and late spring to enjoy the seasonal changes. Paul usually joins me on one of my visits. Eunice and her husband, Archie, coincided their visits to Virginia with mine. We four siblings were always happy to be reunited.

Virginia continues to hold its charm for me. The countryside has retained its beauty. The people are warm and friendly.

I was most proud when Virginia was the first state to elect a black governor, Douglas Wilder.

My happiness was marred by the deaths of other family members. My sister-in-law Doris died in 1975. Her two wishes had been fulfilled: that she lived to see all four of her sons finish college, two with medical degrees; the other was to see her granddaughter, Crystal, born.

My mother died in 1979 at the age of 94. I was able to be with her a few weeks before her death. She appeared to have clung to life until she had seen all her descendants. She had been the last survivor in her family.

The family had increased by the end of 1983. Three of Harold's sons married and his sons, Wayne and Steven each had two children.

My daughter Enid divorced and married Warren Simmons, Ph. D. They had a son who bears part of my father's name, Nicholas Maxville. A perfect child in every aspect, he was born at a time when I welcomed another progeny. My parents' descendants now numbered twelve.

The family circle was broken again in 1982 with the death of my brother-in-law Archie Le Cesne. At the time of his death he was a retired superior court judge. Two of his nephews are Bryant Gumbel of N.B.C. televised "Today Show" and Greg Gumbel, the sports commentator. Bryant had been sent on assignment and was unable to attend the funeral. Greg came and gave a tribute to him saying he assumed a father role for his family after the death of his father, Judge Richard Gumbel.

As we grow older Nature somehow lessens the pain and grief of losing a loved one. I suppose this is a way to ease our fears and accept our own mortality.

When my cousin Fabian Labat died, I helped his sons with funeral arrangements.

I was able to see our dear friend, John Thomas Martin, two days before his demise and thank him for contributing to my happiness.

"You deserved it, doll," was his response.

I have made my desire known to my family that I want to be carried back to Virginia to the family graveyard for my final resting place.

My twilight years have been my best years. All my descendants have fulfilled my aspirations.

My daughter, Enid, is now Program Manager in the U.S. Department of Education. My granddaughter, Stacey, graduated from Princeton and received an MBA from Wharton School of

Business. She is now in international investment banking with Solomon Brothers of New York City.

Robert is now in the second year of the master's program at Northwestern University in film making.

I have lived a blissful life in California. I was visiting my family in Washington each time the two catastrophes occurred in California, the 1989 earthquake and the Oakland Hill's fire in 1991, which spared me from experiencing these catastrophic events.

We joined a country club where I learned to play golf and we travel extensively. I live an integrated life with friends of diverse races.

I am disturbed that the recent verdict of the O.J. Simpson trial referred to by the media as "the trial of the century" has exposed the sharp division of the races.

I viewed the televised Million Black Men's march in Washington orchestrated by Louis Farrakhan, Minister of the Nation of Islam. The purpose of this march was for the atonement of past sins, to inspire black men to accept more responsibilities and self renewal by appealing to their deep need for self-respect and self-empowerment.

I was proud that my grandson, Robert, participated. It will now be up to him to take up the gauntlet of protest against injustices which began in my family with my father. I have been fortunate to live to hold Robert's children, my great granddaughter and great-grandson, in my arms.

Three years ago I visited Jamestown. In reading about the history of the area, I learned for the first time that the Africans who came in 1619 were not sold as slaves to the white settlers but were classified as indentured servants to serve a specific time to pay for their passage to the Colony. My curiosity was aroused. Could the history I learned in high school and college be wrong? Is it possible that some of the Nickens ancestors began their lives here? I became determined to continue the search of our family roots that were begun by my sister Elizabeth.

Fig.17 Papa holding his grandson, Wayne.

Fig.18 Family members at first Nickens-Colvin Reunion. L-R: Mama; Papa's youngest sister, Katie Nickens Colvin; first Nickens grandchild, Estelle Labat; and Elizabeth Colvin Tapscott.

Fig. 19 Present Virginia home; replaced original farm house.

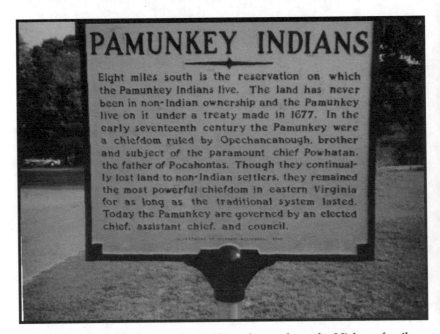

Fig. 20 Reservation of Pamunkey Indians from whom the Nickens family are descended.

Fig. 21 Two Generations: Seated, My mother. Standing, My brother, J. Harold Nickens, M.D.; My sister, Elizabeth Nickens; My sister, Eunice LeCesne; and Me.

Fig. 22 Four Generations: Front Row, L-R, Husband, Paul; sister, Eunice LeCesne; me; grandson's wife, Staci Muhammad, holding my great granddaughter, Sharriah. Back Row, L-R, granddaughter, Stacey Herndon; grandson, Nicholas Simmons; daughter, Enid Simmons, grandson; grandson, Robert Muhammad.

Fig. 23 My great grandchildren, Sharriah and Mikkail Muhammad.

Fig. 24 Family at my sister Elizabeth's memorial.

Fig. 25 Family gathered at naming of Elizabeth Nickens Park, Haymarket, Virginia, in memory of my sister. 1999.

Fig. 26 My California Lunch Bunch Club.

Fig. 27 Senator and Mrs. Edward Brooke at the Smart Set Conclave.

Fig. 28 D.C. Friends celebrating my birthday

Fig. 29 National Smart Set members attending a Conclave.

Chapter Fifteen

The Nickens Family — Three Hundred Years of Freedom

Negro blood is sure powerful because just one drop of black
blood makes a colored man.
One drop — you are a Negro.
Black is powerful.

—Langston Hughes, 1953

Colonial Era

The words of my paternal grandmother made an indelible impression on me when she admonished us, "Remember, tell your children that their grandfather's people were never slaves."

At the time I began this book about my family and a chronicle of my life, I began my search of the genealogical roots of the Nickens family prior to 1800. My sister, Elizabeth, had established through her research that our great, great grandmother Sally Nickens was born free in 1799 as well as her brothers, Barney, born in 1800, and Reuben, born in 1802.

The family also possessed sections of a book by Luther Jackson listing several Nickens Negro men who fought in the Revolutionary War. I was curious to learn if any of these veterans were our forebears.

I began my quest in the genealogical section of the Library of Congress where I read several references that refuted works of early historians that the first Negroes arriving in America were slaves. After reviewing six books written by various historians, I felt I had sufficient evidence that these first black Jamestown arrivals as well as many of those blacks who arrived in the next four decades were not classified as slaves.

The first Jamestown Negroes were not free, however; instead they fell into a category of indentured servants who bound themselves to work for masters for a specified length of time in return for paying the cost of their transportation across the Atlantic from the West Indies.

At the end of a servant's period the master had to give him freedom dues: clothing, a small amount of money, and a plot of land—an expense never incurred with slaves.

During the first half century of its existence, Virginia had many Negro indentured servants, and the records reveal an increasing number of free Negroes. (Franklin and Moss 1947:53). They had Spanish names: Antoney, Isabella, Pedro. The first black settlers accumulated land, voted, testified in court and mingled with whites on an equal basis. There were skilled farmers and artisans among the first African Americans. (Bennett 35,36)

With this information, I embarked on a search to determine if any of our ancestors were direct descendants of these early Negro settlers.

After months researching records in the Mormon Temple, the Virginia Historical Societies, census records, and ship logs of Colonial America, I was unsuccessful in identifying any free Nickens family listed in the Colonial era.

I was discouraged when I sought information regarding free Negroes at the National Archives and was told by an uninformed librarian there were no free Negroes in Virginia after the 1700's because they had all been imported out of Virginia. She was referring to several petitions to the Virginia legislature which demanded the removal of all free Negroes from Virginia. I disputed the librarian's information and told her these laws were never enforced because the free Negroes had no place to go. Nevertheless, she refused to help me find information on the subject of Virginia's free Negroes.

Several months later fate was kinder; my cousin, Dr. Herbert Nickens, received a call from a Lizzel Copeland. She told him she had selected his name out of the phone directory. She explained she was a Nickens descendent researching her Nickens roots. She was curious to learn if the two branches of Nickens had common ancestors. I was given her phone number and was able to talk directly to her.

She gave me the name of a book she had found in the National Archives, *Evolution of A Southern Tidewater Community, Lancaster, Virginia 1650-1750* by Robert Anthony Wheeler, 1978.

The book mentions a will of John Carter from Lancaster, Virginia, written in 1690. In this will he frees Chriss and Black Dick. Why were these persons relevant to our family's history? Their children had the surname Nickens.

My nephew, Dr. J. Harold Nickens, Jr. made several trips to the Lancaster County Courthouse and the Northumberland County Library to search records pertaining to the Nickens family. In the Lancaster County Office of Wills he obtained a copy of John Carter's will which reads:

In The Name of God Amen.

I John Carter being sick of body but sound an perfect memory doe make this my last will & testament. I bequeath my soule to the Almighty God hopeing that God Almighty will wash away my sins by the blood of Jesus Christ my dear Saviour trusting through his merritorious satisfaction I shall be called to Everlasting Glory. And my Wordly Estate I doe despose of as followeth:

First. I doe give Black Dick and Chriss his Wife after the finishing of the Crop that is now on the grounds their Freedom, and I doe give each of them a Cow and Calfe and three barrels of Corn a peece, and I doe give of them so much ground upon the land I bought of Nicholas Wren and old Clapham, for their lives so they may tend with houses convient for them and timber for casques. And Likewise Chrisses youngest Daughter, I set free along with her and likewise I doe give Diana and Little Chriss their freedom when they come to the age of eighteen and that they meantime remain with my Wife. And I doe give each of them a yearling heifer with their increase until they come to half a dozen to run along with my wife's stock of cattle.

I pondered as to why he mentioned freeing Chriss and Dick even before mentioning his children. Further in the will he mentions his "Negroes."

Item. My Will is that the Land I bought of William Clapham bee continued seated with tenn negroes for the use of my Childe until the day of her marriage.

Item. I give unto my Daughter, Elizabeth, the negro Childe Bridget to waite upon her.

Item. I give unto my Granddaughter Ann Jones a Negro wench between the age of fifteen years and twenty.

Item. To Son William Negro man, Harry.

Daughter Lucy - Negro boy Simon and Negro woman Rose.

Daughter, Francina - Negro boy Sam and Negro girl Hazar.

To Elizabeth Nickens - a heiffer three years old.

Elizabeth is the daughter of Chriss and Dick. The court records list Chriss and Dick as both being born in 1660. The names of their children listed in Lancaster County Court records were:

Edward born 1680

Ely born 1682

William born 1685

Chriss, Jr. born 1690

Diana no birthdate but mentioned in Carter's will.

There are several reasons to conclude that Dick and Chriss were not slaves but were indentured servants.

One, their marriage was recorded in 1679. Slaves did not officially marry; they performed marriage rituals on the plantation, such as jumping over a broomstick. Although such marriages were permitted and recognized by their masters they were not recorded in church nor court records.

Two, they were given freedom "dues" which slaves did not receive.

Third, they were baptized which prevented them from being classified as slaves at that time.

Four, they were born in 1660, two years before the first slave act was enacted.

Black Dick first appeared on the tax lists in 1699 and was listed as follows:

1699 Black Dick 1 tithe

1700 Black Dick 4 tithes

1701 Free Dick 1 tithe

1702 Free Dick 1 tithe

1703 Free Richard 1 tithe

1704 Richard Yoconhanocan 1 tithe

1706 Free Dick 1 tithe

Yoconohanocan is an Indian name. The Pamunkey and Rappahamock tribes occupied that Virginia area, which leads me to believe that Richard Yoconohanocan was an Indian and reclaimed his tribal name.

Helen Roundtree writes in her book *Pocahontas People* that young Indians were called "black boys" which explains why Richard was referred to as Black Dick.

The Treaty of Middle Plantation in 1677 between the Pamunkey tribe and the white settlers stipulated that Indian servants were to serve for as long as English indentured servants did and they were not to be enslaved by their employers.

This gives further evidence that Black Dick was not a slave but an indentured servant.

Several sources, particularly Helen Roundtree, have stated that Indians were arbitrarily classified as Negro through the 1700's and 1800's. Sentiment ran very high against Indians in Colonial Virginia and several attempts were made to exterminate them. Fearing for their lives, many Indians identified themselves as Negroes or mulattoes.

Two of Richard Yoconohanocan's sons were listed on the tax rolls.

1707 Ely Yocohoc paid 2 tithes

1709 Edward Yockonhawken paid 1 tithe

Attention is called to the difference in spelling of the two brother's surnames.

1710 Edward was listed as Edward Nocan which is the last part of Yoconohanocan. Later he appeared on the tax rolls as Edward Nickens. One conjecture is the Indian name was too long and too difficult for the recorder to spell thus the name eventually evolved to Nickin, then to Nicken, then Nickens.

Nickens is an English name; however, no whites were listed by the surname Nickens in Virginia in the early 1700's. This proves that our family name was not taken from a slave master but was derived from an Indian name.

Edward was not listed as a Negro until 1715. This probably due to his racially mixed parentage: Indian, white and black.

Historians indicate almost from the time blacks arrived in Virginia there were interracial sexual relations between Indians and those of black ancestry and white ancestry. As there was a scarcity of white women, there was far more sexual contact between the English men and black women than between white women and black men. A mulatto population was emerging, resulting from racial mixing.

Ira Berlin in *Slaves Without Masters* writes, "The number of free Negroes were seldom met with. The few free persons of color that were in the colonies were chiefly mulattoes, the children of white settlers."

Chriss was probably a mulatto. A mulatto was defined as a person whose parents were of black and white racial mixtures.

Beginning in 1660, Virginia enacted harsher laws that prolonged the indenture of Negroes.

A 1681 law declared that children born of white women and free black women would be free.

The 1691 statute (Act XV) was designed to prevent Negroes, mulattoes and Indians intermarrying with English or other white women.

As the free Negroes and slaves developed more Caucasoid characteristics, the slave masters in Virginia adopted the one-sixteenth rule which meant any person who had a great, great, great, great ancestor of African descent was classified as a Negro. Later the one-drop rule was adopted defining a Negro as someone with any African ancestry. The purpose was to increase the slave population to provide more free labor for the planters.

The end of indentured servitude resulted in fewer mulattoes being born to white women; by the middle of the eighteenth century, most racially mixed children were fathered by planters, sons of planters, and overseers.

The children of Chriss and Dick, being free, prospered economically. Edward is listed as a householder for at least eleven years and a landowner who paid taxes on fifty acres of land in Christ Church Parish in 1714 and sold this land on 20 March 1722 [11:212-3]. He was called a "free Negro" in Lancaster County lists of tithables. On November 2, 1722 he purchased 40 acres on the west side of Corrotoman River [11:222-23] and another 50 acres adjoining this land and land of Robert Carter on 13 September 1726. He sold this land on 5 March 1730 [12:147-9]. His 21

September 1735 Lancaster will was proved on 12 November the same year (see appendix).

His wife, Mary, and his children listed in his will were: sons Tun, Robert, Edward, Richard and James; daughters were Sarah and Aner.

His son James is named in Court Orders of Lancaster County dated in 1739.

James Nickens, Orphan of Edward Nickens; died, is by the Court bound to John Hubbard till he attains the age of twenty-one years. The said John is to teach him to read and write and the trade of a shoemaker and to fund and allow him sufficient and cleanly diet, lodging, and apparel and at the expiration of his servitude to pay him as is appointed for servants by indenture or custom —

This James Nickens, born around 1730, is the direct ancestor of my Nickens family line. This has been substantiated by Karen Sutton in her Genealogy Genogram, *The Nickens Family: Tracing Non-Slave African Americans.*

Karen Sutton is a member of another branch of the Nickens families. She is the only legitimate African American member of the D.A.R. She has documented and traced her family line to Amos Nickens who fought in the Revolutionary War. I received a copy of the Genealogy Genogram she has done on my family line.

James is listed in Virginia records as married to Margaret Carter. He was a land owner in Potecasi Creek Society Parish, Bertie County, by deed of gift from his wife's parents.

Up to the time James reached adulthood the free Negroes enjoyed many of the same civil rights as whites after their indentured servitude. More restrictions were imposed on free Negroes after Virginia enacted stricter slave laws. To begin with, color indicated condition: if one had dark skin, he had to prove he was not a slave. All free persons had to carry a certificate of freedom paper issued by the County Court giving the person's name, stature, complexion, and any other identification mark and how his freedom was obtained. If he or she lost their papers, they could be sold on the block as a slave.

They were not permitted to own firearms unless by special permit. They could not vote nor hold public office. They could not assemble except in church. Marriage between whites and Negroes were forbidden.

Lancaster County, Virginia, is a small county in size. The Nickens families resided in this area for three generations. They were a closely-knit family and were well known by the white plantation owners and other small white farmers.

Because of the oppressive and discriminatory laws, free Negroes turned to similar free persons and separated themselves from those living in poverty; mulattoes refused to associate with blacks. Most free Negroes living in close proximity with whites maintained good relations with their neighbors. As I noted in an earlier chapter, they were forbidden to associate with slaves because whites considered them to be subversive and liable to arouse insurrections among slaves.

Luther Jackson writes of the Nickens family in an article, "Free Negroes of Petersburg, Virginia," *Journal of Negro History, XII*. Many of them married legally; they bound out their children as apprentices to learn trades, and to learn to read, write and cipher; some engaged in law suits as plaintiffs and defendants. Several bought and conveyed property by deed and by will.

Possessing a long history of literacy passed from one generation to the other enabled them to write and record their wills and interpret their land deeds.

They worked hard at their trades, accumulating enough money to buy their farms. I presume they assisted each other at planting and harvesting times, their wives gathering to quilt, preserve and dry foods for the winter. They associated freely with the Indians, joining their pow-wows and in turn the

Indians attending their feasts. They set snares to catch game for food since few were allowed to own guns. They fished in the Rappohanick and caught crabs in the Chesapeake.

Whites permitted them to attend church services and baptize their children in Christ Church Parish.

They read the posters at the Court house concerning the approaching war and the imminent revolt of the colonies.

The information accrued regarding the Colonial Nickens families causes me to pause and imagine what life was like for them during that era. Neither slave nor completely free, neither black nor white, neither poor nor wealthy, they functioned as a third element in a system built for two.

Lancaster County where they resided is a small county in area, located in southeastern Virginia and bounded on the south and east by the Chesapeake Bay and on the west by the Rappohanick River. Indians lived on reservations edging the river. All the Nickens clan lived within a few miles of each other.

Revolutionary War and Post-War Period

The name James appears to be the most popular first name in the Nickens families. For seven generations there was a James in our family line.

The first James, Edward's son, was probably named for King James II of England who ruled the colonies at that time. He had a son James, Jr. born in 1753.

As the war approached, land available for sale to free Negroes became scarce. Slave owners had their slaves learn the trades and hired them out to work and to work on their plantations. This lessened the employment for the free men.

When the Revolutionary War began, Negroes free and slave were excluded. As the war entered the third year of 1777, Congress reversed this policy and free Negroes were recruited to join the army and navy. At first the slave holder sent his slaves to fight in his place as quotas for each state were set. The British promised all slaves would be free if they joined their side. This promise was kept even after the British Army was defeated, which increased the number of free Negroes.

Several Nickens men joined not only for patriotic reasons but because they were promised a bounty in land and money.

From the Revolutionary Roster of Soldiers and Seamen are the names of Nickens men who were all related:

Nickens, Amos Northumberland Seaman
Nickens, Edward Lancaster Seaman
Nickens, Hezekiah Lancaster Seaman
Nickens, James Jr. Lancaster Seaman &Soldier

Nickens, John Lancaster Seaman
Nickens, Nathaniel Lancaster Seaman
Nickens, Richard Lancaster Soldier
Nickens, William Lancaster Soldier

The James Nickens, Jr. listed as seaman and soldier was the son of James, the youngest son of Edward and our direct ancestor. This Revolutionary War hero was married to Sally. Their four children were Hezekiah, James, Elizabeth and Judy.

The following excerpts are from Karen Sutton's Genealogy Genogram, *The Nickens Family: Tracing Non Slave African Americans:*

FAMILY GROUP RECORD-78
DOCUMENTATION

28 Aug 1995   Page 5 of 5

HUSBAND James NICKEN-219   Yr of Birth

WIFE   Yr of Birth

UPDATE: 1994-02-02

Served in the Revolutionary War. Testifies that he is a Free Man of Color, aged about Fifty-five on 27 April 1818. That he served in the Revolutionary War for three years on board the Ships *Tempest, Revenge* and *Hero*. After discharge from the Navy he enlisted in the Land Service of the War at Lancaster Court House in Virginia.

On 16 August 1820, he testifies that he enlisted under Capt. Nicholas Currell at Lancaster Court House, and was marched from Lancaster Court House by Currell to the Headquarters of Barron Steuben, then at Cumberland Courthouse, there he was placed under the command of Drury Ragsdale and Flemming Gaines commanding a Company belonging to Col. Harrison's Regiment of Artillery.

Excerpts from Revolutionary War Pension and Bounty Land Warrant Application Files, Microcopy 804, Roll 1821 —

Va James Nickens S38262

Transcribed at National Archives, Washington, DC on 1 Feb 1994, in Microfilm Room — 4th Floor

Page 1 NGS Index Nickens, James Va., S38262

Microcopy 881, Roll 1094 Compiled Service Records of Soldiers Who served in the Revolutionary War.

FAMILY GROUP RECORD-79
DOCUMENTATION

28 Aug 1995   Page 4 of 9

HUSBAND James NICKENS Sr. -235   Yr of Birth 1753

WIFE Sally NICKENS-234   Yr of Birth

Vol. 175; page 69

J.W. Wilkinson
copyist

Revolutionary War Pension and Bounty Land Warrant Application Files Microcopy 804, Roll 1821 — Nickins, James

NARA 1969

Va Nickins, James S38262
   or Nickens

Revolutionary War Pension and Bounty Land Warrant Application Files Microcopy 804, Roll 1820 NARA 1969

(living in Stafford County) Free Man of Color aged about Fifty-Five (on 27 April 1818) served in Revolutionary War for three years on Board the Ships Tempest, Revenge and Hero. After discharge enlisted in the Land Service for the War at Lancaster Court House in Virginia.

16 August 1820—appears in Court enlisted under Capt. Nicholas Currell at Lancaster Court House, and was marched by Currell to Headquarters of Barron Steuben, then at Cumberland Courthouse, then placed under command of Drury Ragsdale and Flemming Gaines commanding a Company belonging to Col. Harrison's Regiment of Artillery.

FAMILY GROUP RECORD-79
DOCUMENTATION

28 Aug 1995   Page 2 of 9

HUSBAND: James NICKENS, SR.-235   Yr of Birth 1753

WIFE: Sally NICKENS-234   Yr of Birth

HUSBAND - James NICKENS Sr.-235

UPDATE: 1994-09-11

Death Date from "Memorial of the Heirs" found in Pension Records for State of VA for the Revolutionary War. Also name and approximate death date of wife, and names of children. Obtained from VSLA, Richmond, VA 03 Sept. 1994

Full text follows:

Virginia. At a court continued and held for Frederick County the 3rd day of September 1834.

It is ordered to be certified that it appears to the Court by satisfactory evidence that James Nickens who served in the Virginia State Navy in the Revolutionary War died about the year 1825 and that Sally Nickens, his wife, James Nickens his son and Elizabeth Nickens and Judy Nickens his daughters were all, and his only heirs at Law at the time of his death: that the said Sally Nickens the widow has since died without further issue; and that the said James Nickens, Elizabeth Nickens, and Judy Watkins are now the only heirs at law of the said James Nickens who served in the Virginia State Navy as aforesaid.

It is ordered to be certified that it appears to the Court by satisfactory evidence that Hezekiah Nickens who served in the Virginia State Navy in the Revolutionary War died during the revolutionary war, and that James Nickens his father, James Nickens, Elizabeth Nickens, and Judy Watkins his brother and sisters were his only heirs at Law at the time of his death; that the said James Nickens Senr. has since died leaving Sally

Nickens his widow and the said James Nickens Jr. Elizabeth Nickens and Judy Watkins his only heirs at Law at the time of his death.

That the said Sally Nickens has since died without further issue than the children of James Nickens Senr. aforesaid: and that the said James Nickens Jr. Elizabeth Nickens and Judy Watkins are now the only heirs at Law of the aforesaid Hezekiah Nickens who served in the Virginia State Navy as aforesaid.

I Thomas Allen Tobalt clerk of the Court of the County aforesaid do hereby certify that the foregoing are transcripts from the records of my office.

In testimony whereof I have hereunto set my hand and affixed the seal of said court this 6th day of January 1836 and in the 60th year of the Commonwealth.

Thomas Tobalt clk

After discharge from the Navy, James enlisted in the Land Service of the War at Lancaster Courthouse in Virginia.

The government granted the Revolution War veterans land in the state of Ohio where few Nickens family members settled. Most traded their Ohio land for land adjoining Lancaster County. They seemed to prefer living near each other.

There is some question about Hezekiah being James' son because of the closeness in their ages. He is listed as having been killed in the Revolutionary War; his heirs were listed as James, Elizabeth, and Judy, his siblings. Perhaps he was very young and served as an officer's boy.

During the post-Revolution period, the Nickens families survived on their war pensions. The men were prevented from working in the skilled trades, because they were replaced by slaves learning and working these crafts. Consequently they were not as prosperous as their early free ancestors. Some moved near towns where they acquired jobs as coachmen or tavern workers. For this reason free men of color were not as financially able to provide for their families as their ancestors had been.

Free Negro women were likely not to be married, even though they headed households and had children. Here the law limited their chances, for slaves could not legally marry, and interracial marriages were out of bounds. This was mentioned in Chapter V, "My Family and Extended Family."

The Revolutionary War hero, James, my forefather, died in 1825 in Frederick County, Virginia. His son, James III, born in 1775 in Lancaster County, moved to Culpepper County, Virginia, as an adult where he married Peggy Bearden. His children were Sally Ann, and two sons, Reuben and Barney.

The previous research of the Nickens family by my sister Elizabeth established that the Sally Ann listed was our great, great grandmother. These statistics enabled me to complete the Nickens family tree proving my grandmother's words to be true, "The Nickens family were never slaves." Our lineage spanned over three hundred years of freedom in America.

I will leave it to future female Nickens descendants as to whether they wish to pursue membership in the Daughters of American Revolution.

At the completion of our genealogical research I had a strong desire to visit Africa. I was anxious to see if I felt any relatedness to my African ancestors as I had for my English forbears during my stay in England.

Paul and I took a cruise that began in South Africa. I felt some relatedness to the Coloreds. These people reminded me of my free people of color, whose rights were previously denied and who lived in a segregated area inferior to whites. The interracial mixture and physical appearance were similiar to my family.

Our cruise took us to small island settlements off Madagascar and then to Tanzania. It was in Zanzibar, Tanzania, where I learned of the strong family unity of Africans. Large apartments were occupied by members of the same family, parents, aunts, uncles, etc. This form of extended family living reminded me of the Nickens family members who lived in apartments in the Ringwood house and some who built homes on Ringwood land, forming a family compound.

It was in this city where we visited the slave mart. The guide described how the captured slaves were yoked together and forced to walk several miles before arriving at the slave marts to be sold. The marts contained dungeons where the slaves were kept until they were sold, branded and put on ships to cross the infamous Middle Passage.

In these dungeons the men and women were separated. The children were put with their mothers. They were chained to each other and held in a space no higher than eighteen inches. A pit in the floor served as their toilet that they were allowed to use at certain intervals; otherwise, they had to lie in their human excrement if they had dysentery.

The marts were similar on the east coast of Africa. President Clinton used the slave trading mart on Senegal's Garee Island as the backdrop when he apologized for slavery during his 1998 African tour.

My feelings of revulsion overcame me and I told Paul I had to leave before I became ill. Was this where some of my ancestors were held and later sold and brought to America, where they were again sold? Only the strongest could survive this form of torture. I took some consolation in the fact that most did survive and perhaps it is their genes I have inherited, which have allowed me to reach longevity in excellent physical and mental health.

When I considered which people were responsible for this inhumane treatment of these Africans I reviled all three groups: the African tribal leader who sold captured Africans and some of his own people in return for trinkets; the slave trader, and the American slave owners who kept humans in bondage for one hundred-eighty-three years.

We continued our cruise to Kenya where I found the natives to be friendly and hard-working people. At each country we visited they performed beautiful rhythmic dances in costume. I ate one African meal and was amazed at the similarity of the entrees to our "soul food" or Southern cooking. Then the thought occurred to me that the cooks on the plantations brought their method of cooking from Africa. Unfortunately, I later became ill because my stomach could not digest the palm oils used in frying.

My nephew, J. Harold Nickens, has done intensive research of our Indian heritage. He has become knowledgeable and familiar with many of the people and their culture. He attends their pow-wows regularly and makes artifacts relating to their customs.

He located some Indians with the last name Nickens, who live in North Carolina and Tennessee, with whom he has formed a friendship. Last summer two men from that family visited him and he brought them to visit Eunice and me during our stay in Virginia. They said their mother's maiden name was Nickens. They were warm and friendly and kissed us upon leaving.

J. Harold took Eunice and me to a pow-wow while we were in Virginia, where we observed the different skin colors which indicated they were racially mixed with black and white. Their costumes were elaborate works of art. Their dances were primitive, unlike the rhythmic African dances. I was never a good dancer and wished I had inherited the natural bodily rhythms of my African ancestors. I am thankful that my African genes have endowed me with melanin in my skin which has prevented extreme wrinkling and for the natural curl in my hair.

There is a saying that you do not know who you are until you know from whence you came.

After researching my roots, I know from whence I came. I came from people who were English aristocrats who migrated to this country and who claimed land granted them by their king. I came from poor Irish immigrants seeking to improve economically. I came from free people of African descent who came to this land, were classified as indentured servants and who fought in a war to make this country free. I came from people brought to America from Africa in chains, whose free labors helped to make this a rich country. I came from Native American people who originally owned this land.

Who am I? I am not a European American, nor an African American, nor an American Indian (or native American).

I AM AN AMERICAN!!!

Family Legacy

This chapter is devoted to the third generation of our parents and to all future generations who will read this book.

I had hoped you would reap the benefits that our forefathers struggled, fought, and died for in order to make this a better country and world for you and your descendants.

I am perturbed that as we enter the twenty-first century the American dream is endangered and the future is filled with uncertainty.

The conservative idealogy of right wing partisans are pushing legislation to reverse the gains made by ethnic minorities and women by eliminating affirmative action which gave preferences in hiring and similar situations to groups that had suffered in the past from discrimination.

Our clean air environment is being threatened by their vote to remove restrictions from the Environmental Protection Agency. Due to the changes in the economic conditions of the country and the world, you can no longer take for granted that you will live better economically than your parents.

The emergence of racism and the divisiveness of the races will adversely affect the good-will and race relations that have existed for the last twenty-five years.

Let not your hearts be troubled by these negative messages but hold fast to your dreams and find hope in the fact that we came from a long line of people who endured far worse than what you must now deal with in modern America.

Some of our ancestors survived the indignities and evils of slavery while others who were always free endured oppressive discriminatory laws inflicted on them and some were harassed and driven off their land.

We did not inherit a vast amount of material wealth from our parents, but the intrinsic values they instilled in us and which we passed on to you will carry you much further in life toward becoming more productive citizens, an asset to your community, and succeeding in living rich and fulfilling lives.

What are the intrinsic values that are our parent's legacy to you?

1. The importance of pursuing and achieving education that will allow you to reach your highest potential. Knowledge is power.

2. The power you derive by your vote in local and national elections, which can effect change in unfair and unjust laws.

3. Exercising your freedom of speech by writing to the media and your congressmen and by participating in peaceful protests against injustices.

4. Exhibiting tolerance and assistance to your less-fortunate fellow beings.

5. Assuming responsibility of rearing and caring for your families.

6. Adhering to moral and ethical virtues.

7. Belief in a higher Being or Creator.

8. They leave you the gift of their love for it was this love that saw us through the tough times and built our self esteem that prevented us from feeling inferior to anyone.

9. You have inherited a high level of intelligence which family members have proven by their outstanding academic achievements and successful professional careers. Those of you who have yet to complete your education are a source of family pride by continuing to receive academic honors. This family of high achievers debunks the theory of the recent book, *The Bell Curve,* authored by

Herrnstein and Murry who espoused the theory that
blacks are innately mentally inferior to other races.

The only tangible value is the Virginia land which you will
eventually inherit making you the sixth generation to own this
land. This land that has served to keep our family united, bring
peace to our lives, provide us with a sense of security, and continue family traditions. Avoid holding it if it impedes progress.
Do not let the division and sale of the land cause bitterness between you and other family members.

It was encumbered on our predecessors to perpetuate
colorism which enabled them to receive preferential treatment
from both white and black races on the basis of their skin color.
You now live in an enlightened society and are free and encouraged to love and admire persons for their inner and physical
beauty regardless of the color of their skin and the texture of
their hair.

Be proud of the Nickens name you bear and the Nickens
blood that flows through your veins. Always remember that
some of your people were in this land before many Europeans,
Asians or Hispanics. No matter what label, racial category, or
classification others assign to you, know within yourselves you
are a mixture of three races and should consider yourselves
Americans of color.

Epilogue

My brother, James Harold Nickens, Sr., M.D., died in December, 1995, while I was on my African trip. I attended his memorial upon my return.

My sister, Elizabeth Estelle Nickens, died October 29, 1996. A park located in Haymarket, Virginia, has been named for her, in gratitude for her strong activism and service in the community.

Neither my brother nor sister lived to read this book.

Appendix One

Deed, Wills, and Court Records
Lancaster County Wills 1690-1709

John Carter's Transcribed Will

pp.
3-
5

IN THE NAME OF GOD Amen, I JOHN CARTER being sick of body but of sound and p:fect memory doe make this my last Will & Testament. Imprs. I bequeath my Soule to the Almighty God hopeing that God Almighty will wash away my Sins by the blood of Jesus Christ my dear Saviour trusting that through his merritorious satisfacon I shall bee comitted up into Everlasting Glory. And my worldly Estate I doe despose of as followeth:

·First. I doe give Black Dick and Chriss his Wife after the finishing of the Crop that is now on the Grounde their Freedom, and I doe give each of them a Cow and Calfe and three barrells of Corn a peece, and I doe likewise give them so much ground upon the Land I bought of NICHOLAS WREN and old CLAPHAM, for their lives so they may tend with houses convenient for them and timber for casques, And Likewise Chrisses youngest Daughter, I set free along with her, and likewise, I doe give Diana and Little Chriss: their Freedom when they come to the age of Eighteen yeres, and that they in the meantime remaine with my Wife, And I doe give each of them a yearling heifer with their encrease until they come to halfe a dozen to run along with my Wifes stock of cattle, and all the rest of theire encrease I give unto my Wife:

Item. I give unto EDWARD HERBERT, Twenty shillings to buy him a Ring. I give alsoe unto the said EDWARD HERBERT all my wearsing apparrell;

Item. I give unto my Wife in lieu of full satisfaccon of the Joynture I made to her before marriadge, one third part of my p:sonall Estate here in Virginia after the debts paide, what is due from the Estate the Tobacco now groving hence excepted but if my Wife bee not content with what I have here given her in my Will, but shall sue for more, then my Will is that the Gift bee voide and that she have noe more but the Joynture I made her before marriadge;

Item. I give unto my Wife the two Saddle Horses she brought along with her.

Item. I give unto my Wife one third part of all the bookes of Divinity, the other two thirds of the bookes of Divinity I give to my Daughter, ELIZABETH;

Item. After my debts paide, I give the other two thirds of my p:sonall Estate here in Virginia unto my Daughter, ELIZABETH, and my Will is that this Crop now goeing home bee consigned to Mr. EDWARD LEMAN and Mr. ARTHUR BALEY, all the money I have in England with the p:duce of this saide Cropp I give unto my Daughter, ELIZABETH, except my Brother, CHARLES's, Portion which is to bee paide out of the saide money:

Johns Carter's transcribed will

Item. My Will is that the Land I bought of WILLIAM CLAPHAM and NICHOLAS WREN bee continued seated with tenn Negroes for the use of my Childe untill the day of her marriage or till she bee of the age of eighteen yeares which shall happen first and that then she have full power to dispose of her selfe and her Estate as she pleases;

Item. I give unto my Daughter, ELIZABETH, the Negro Childe Bridget to waite upon her;

Item. I give unto my Daughter her owne Mothers rideing horse. My Will is that what money my Daughter shall have in England bee put out to Interest for her use by Mr. EDWARD LEMAN and Mr. ARTHUR BALEY, with good security for the amount of the principall when she shall come of age or at marriage;

Secondly, I give unto my Sons, FRANCIS and WILLIAM EMANUELL, all the Land that I am now possest withall to bee equally shared and devided when my youngest Sone comes to age to them and their heires forever only it is my Wil that my Daughters shall have previledge to live and remaine in the House along with: their Brothers untill they bee married and then to have ground to worke for their living not depending upon their Brothers for maintenance;

Thirdly, I give unto my Daughter, HONOUR, one heifer with calfe with her increase forever,

Fourthly, I give unto my Daughter, ANIE EMANUELL, one cowe called by the name of Nell with her encrease forever;

Fifthly, I give unto my Daughter, KATHARINE EMANUELL one cowe called by the name of Young Star with her encrease forever.

Sixthly, I give unto my Daughter, MARGARET EMANUELL, the first mare colt that either of my mares bring with her encrease forever;

Seventhly, I give unto my two Sones, FRANCIS and WILLIAM EMANUELL, my two mares and two horses, only it is my Will that the two mares shall bee let loose and run for breeders and all the mare Colts that the saide mares doe bring shall returne to my Daughters, that is to say, the first to my Daughter, HONOUR, and the second to my Daughter, MARY, and the third to my Daughter, ANIE, and the fourth to my Daughter, KATHARINE, and for my Daughter, MARGARET, it is my Will that she accept of what I have given her by Will as her part and portion;

Eighthly, It is my Will that my Sone, WILLIAM EMANUELL shall live and remaine with HENERY BELL of this Parish untill hee comes of age,

Ninthly, It is my Will that my Sone, FRANCIS EMANUELL, shall imediately possess what is here given him after my decease and also doe appoint him my full and whole Executor;

Tenthly, It is my Will that what household stuffe there is belonging to my House shall not bee moved out of the house but shall remaine tenneantable for the use of all my Children that is willing to live in the Huse and make use of it, And it is also my wish that my Daughter KATHARINE shall live and remaine with JANE REDICK, Widow of this Parish, untill she bee marrigeable, It is also my Will that my Daughter, ANIE EMANU-ELL shall live and remaine with HENERY BELL and his Wife untill three years bee expired from the date of Christmas day last past, And it is also my Will that my Sone whome I have made my Executor shall pay such debts as is just due to pay out of what I have given him and his Brothers not comeing upon his Sisters for any manner of charge; And I doe give unto my two Sones, a pircell of Pipe stands that are transported downe to the Water Side already; And to the intent that this my Will may have due execucon and performance, I have hereunto set my hand and seale the day and date above written

Signed sealed and delivered in the presence of

JOHN BRADLEY.   FRANCIS EMANUELL
WM. BRUSH

Probat. in Cur Com Lancastr: nono die Aprilis 1690   Teste JOHN STRETCHLEY, Cl Cur

Carter's will continued.

Additional Sections of John Carter's Will

[Left to an heir. Name illegible in copy] --negroes Peter and Priscilla, and a childs par
of my household goods and stock.
Son William Jones--all my land situated and being about the falls [illegible]
the Rappahanock, part in the County of King George and part in
Prince William, negro man Harry, and a childs part of my household
goods and stock.
Grandaughter Ann Jones--negro wench between the age of fifteen and
twenty years, to be paid her by my executor at the age of twenty [illegible]
on day of marriage.
All my negroes except Dick (who is to be delivered to my daughter
Elizabeth Bell immediately after my death) to be kept together, and
household goods and stock for the use of my wife and such of the
children as lives with her during her natural life.
Wife, daughter Leeanna Jones, friend the Rev. Mr. John Bell and his
wife Mrs. Elizabeth Bell, and my daughter Ann Jones, and my son
William Jones, executors.
Witness: Henry Lawson, Junr., and Charles Lee.

Page 118a
Craven, Charles, of Wiceccomocc [partially legible] Parish
W.W. 13 September 1740---W.P. 11 May 1741
Wife Rebecka--should have the use of all my estate both real and
personal while a widow.
Daughter Betty and her heirs--plantation whereon I live, negro call
Knail, and the first child my negro Rose brings.
Daughter Lucy--negro boy Simon, and negro woman Rose.
Daughter Francina--negro boy Sam, and negro girl Hazar, and a feather
bed and furniture that is called mine.
Daughter Rhoda--two negro boys Ned and Harry.
Daughter Mary, late wife of William Pasquit, and her heirs--five
schillings sterling.
Four daughters Betty, Lucy, Francina, and Rhoda, should live on my
plantation and their estates as long as they remain unmarried.
Cousin Charles Sullivan--my gun.
To Elizabeth Nickens--a heifer three years old.
Rest of my personal estate at wife's death or marriage, to be equally
divided between my wife and four daughters vizt: Betty, Lucy, Francina,
and Rhoda.
Wife Rebecka, and friend John Coppedge senior, executors.
Witness: George Mills and John Pursley.

Additional sections of Carter's will.

Coppidge, James of Wise Parish
W.W. 23 April 1736 W.P. 13 July 1741
To Godson James Coppidge--tract of land whereon I live, and to the
lawfully begotten heirs of his body. If he should die without such
heirs, the tract of land to go to his brother Moses Coppidge.
To James Coppidge and Moses Coppidge--my negro man Sam, and all my
moveable and personal estate whatsoever.
Brother Charles Coppidge, executor.
Witness: Matthew Zuill, Elizabeth Zuill and David Flicker.

Typed by Historian in Lancaster County from original document.
Re-copied by typist in Alameda County, California.

Final page of Carter's will.

Edward Nickens' will.

Edward Nickens' Will

Lancaster County Virginia Wills 1653-1800

"NICKENS LAST WILL" Deed and Will Book No. 12 1726-1736   Lancaster County, VA p. 355

In the name of God Amen I Edward Nicken of the Parish of Christ Church in Ye County of Lancaster being Sick and weak of Body but in Sound and Good Dispose memory praise be given to god for the Same do make this my Last Will and Testament in manner and forme Following. That is to say, first and principally I Resign my soul into _____ mercifull hands of Almighty god my creator apsured by hopeing through of merits of my Blessed Savior to obtaine _____ of all my sins and my body I commit to the Earth where it was taken to be _____ at ye diferition of my _____ buried and as for the worldly goods hereafter named and Estate Enduring her widowhood and if she maryeth before she dieth then my desire is that my son Jun, and my daughter Sarah and my Son John and my Son Robert and my son Aner may have Equal part of my Estate According to Law, Item I give to my Son Edward Nicken five Shillings and my wife to pay it out of my Estate, Item I give to my son James Nickens five shillings and my wife to pay it out of my Estate. I do appoint my wife Mary Nicken and John Yerby to be my Ex: of my whole Estate Paying my debts and Legacy of this my Last Will and Testament in Witnefs my hand and Seale

21st day of September 1735

                                        Edward Nicken

Signed and Sealed in presence
of us Richard [his mark] Weaver
              mark

Eliza [her mark] Weaver

Simon [his mark X] Shewcraft

At a Court held for Lancaster County on 12th day of Nov 1735 This was proved in open court by the oath of Richard Weaver and Elizabeth Weaver witnefsed thereto and admitted to Record and is Recorded.
                    F. Edwards C Clerk.

```
Edward Nickens' Will

Pp. 360-361   Cash:        10:2:5      3 pr wool 'card
              money scales  0:5:0        1 sugar box        0:5:0
              Pair primges               lines & hooks      0:1:6
              1 Bible & tatter  0:4:0    1 vest & breches o  0:17:9
                                         shirt
              1 Bible       0:3:0        a parcel of small   0:5:3
              a pair of     0:3:6          ware
              old books                  1 small cask        0:3:0
              1 block led               1 old drawing knife  0:1:6
                furniture   1:5:0        1 old hoe o          0:4:0
              4 old blankets  0:12:0     vest o breches

              old flockings
              a pot of feather o 0:50 o
              a dozen o 1/2 bottle  0:3:0    John Meredith
              2 old tables     0:7:0        Wm Hutchings
              1 pr linnen      0:4:0        Thomas Tatt
              7 yds duroy      0:11:0
              10 yds virginia cloth  1:0:0
              4 yds checked linnen  0:5:4
              6 yds course linnen  0:4:6
              1 pr shyllards and    0:8:0
                pea
              1 looking glass   0:2:0
              1 frying pan      0:2:0


              11 February 1735 - apprasment of Estate
              of Edward Nickens, now deceased
```

Additional section of Edward Nickens' will.

Dec . 5 , 1735 - Inventory of Estate of
Edward Nickens

2 sows	0:16:0 lbs.	10 Shoals	1:10:0
A young hog	1:0:0	6 Cows & Calves	10:10:
2 heifers	1:12:6	56g pot Iron	0:14:0
2 other heifers	1:0:0	16 " " "	0:1:4
2 chests	0:14:0	1 Iron Skillet	0:2:0
1 trunk	0:6:0	1 Spit	0:5:0
Bed and furniture	3:10:0	2 wedges	0:2:6
11 ½ hollow pewter	0:19:2	1 Spinning Wheel	0:7:0
15 new pewter	1:0:0	3 Pot hooks	0:5:0
13 ½ old pewter	0:10:1	7 flesh forks & Skimmer	0:3:0
1 old Tankard	0:1:6	1 fire Tongs	0:2:6
2 Dozen Spoons	0:5:0	Barril of Wooden ware	0:8:0
1 Saddle & Bridle	0:19A	2 old tubs	0:4:0
1 Horse	4:0:0	2 Earthen pots	0:0:8
3 Chairs	0:6:0	3 Weeding Hoes	0:5:6
5 ½ Cotton	0:1:4½	4 narrow hoes & axes	0:5:0
9 picked Cotton	0:11:0	1 Broad axe & Slice	0:2:6
3 Stone Jugs	0:4:6	1 Weede an apn & 2 screws	0:4:0
a parcel Earthen Ware	0:6:0	Butchers float	0:2:0
One punch Bowl	0:1:0	7 fathom of rope	0:3:0
1 cyder Cask & tray	0:5:0	1 Iron Pestle	0:3:0

Continuation of Edward Nickens' will.

Original Indenture Document of James Nickens

James Nickin Orphan of Edward Nickins aged is by the Court bound to John Hibbard till he attains the age of twenty one years the said John is to teach him to read & write and the Trade of a shoemaker and to find & allow him sufficient & cleanly diet lodging and apparell and at the expiration of his Indenture to pay him as is appointed for servants by Indenture or Custom ~

ABSTRACTS LANCASTER CO., VA. WILLS 1653-1800
BY
IDA J. LEE

NICKENS, Edward, of Parish of Christ Church. 21 Sept. 1735. Rec. 12 Nov. 1735.
Wife: Mary. Sons: Tun, John, Robert, Edward, Richard, James. Daus: Sarah and Aner. Exors: Wife & John Yerby. Wits: Rich. & Elizabeth Weaver, Simon Shewcraft. W.B. 12, p. 355.

Original Indenture Document of James Nickens.

Lancaster, Co., Va. Court Records 1730-1800

243. 19 September 1716—Betty a negro child the Daughter of Criss, a free negro woman, aged five years old next February is bound to serve Charles Craven his heirs, Executors and Administrators (her said Mother being dead) untill she attaines to the age of eighteen years in Consideration whereof the said Craven doth in Court oblige himself his heirs to cause the said negro Betty to be taught to read the Bible perfectly and during the said term to find and allow her sufficient apparrell and other Christian entertainment suitable to her circumstances. *OB 1713-19, 180.*

41

299. 16 May 1711—This Indenture made and Concluded on and signed the Sixteenth of May in the year of o' Lord one thousand seven hundred and Eleven with and between Henry Tapscott of the above sd County of the one party & Elizabeth Nigings of the County of Lancaster of the other party Witnesseth that the above named Elizabeth Nigings of her own free & Voluntary will hath bound her son Rich⁴ Niggins an Apprentice unto him the said Henry Tapscott & Ann his wife for and during the Terme of fifteen whole years & four months he the sd Richard being six years old next Aug' it is likewise covenanted and agreed that he the said Richard Niggins shall not absent himself day nor night from his said service he shall not play att any unlawfull game as Cards dice whereof his said Master shall sustaine Damage for & during the time of his said Apprenticeship and in Consideration of the True performance of the above mentioned premises the above named Henry Tapscott doe by these presents oblige myself to Learne he the said Richard Niggins to work well att Joyner Carpenter Trade or to doe his honest Endeavo⁷ʳ he the said Richard to help tend Corne for and during the time of his said apprenticeship and in Consideration he the said Henry Tapscott is to Learn he the said Richard Niggins to Read wright to find him in good sufficient Cloathing meat washing and Lodging for & during the time of his said apprenticeship with a new suit of Cloathing and one single sett of Tooles at the Expiration of his said apprenticeship as Witness to the True performance of the above mentioned premises both parties have Interchangeably sett their hand and Seales the day and yeare above written *RB 1710-13, 21.*

her mark
Eliz^ꜣ · Nigings

(1) Indenture of Elizabeth Nickens.
(2) Indenture of Richard Nickens, son of Elizabeth.

I do hereby Certify that I am Willing that Peggy Bearder (Alias Lumber) a free Mulatto who was bound to me should intermarry with James Nikins, both of whom are people of Colour. Given under my hand this 15th day of July 1793

Wm. McClanahan

Teste
Robt Yancey
Robert Latham

A Copy Teste
John Jameson C C Cun

Culpeper County to wit
     This day Wm McClanahan came before me a Justice of the peace for said County and made Oath that Peggy Bearder (Alias Lumber) is a Woman of the Same Colour with James Nickins. Given under my hand this 15th day of July 1793

John Strode

A Copy Teste
John Jameson C C Cun

Marriage license of James Nickens and Peggy Bearden.

GRANTEE	GRANTOR	Book	Page	KIND	_ DATE OF DEED Mo.	Day	Year	DATE OF RECORD Mo.	Day	Year
Nickens, Sally.	Jenkins, George F.	60	152	B & S	Jan	1	1867	Jan 10		1867
Nickens, Sally.	Spilman, Edward M.tee.	63	98	Released	Oct	8	1870	Dec 10		1870
Nickens, Sarah A.& Bernard.	Yeatman, George E.	63	256	B & S	Nov	18	1870	Mar 20		1871
Nickens, Jennie.	Nickens, Sallie.	64	40	B & S	May	6	1871	Nov	8	1871
Nickens, Eliza.	Lee, J.P.& ux.	68	243	B & S	Jul	14	1876	Feb 20		1877
Nickens, Reuben.	Wilson, William B.& ux.	77	427	B & S	Apr	10	1871	Jan 19		1887
Nickens, Mak.	Weaver, A.G.Comr.	84	123	B & S	Feb	4	1893	Aug 28		1893
Nickens, J.M.	Snyder, D.C.& ux.	87	382	B & S	Sep	22	1896	Nov	4	1896
Nickens, Sally	Spilman, E. M. tee	60	152	Trust	1	1	1867	1	10	1867
Nickens, Sallie	Nickens, Jennie	64	40	B & S	5	6	1871	11	8	1871
Nickens, Sarah	Collins, Henry tee for Amanda Collins	66	152	B & S	10	7	1874	10	13	1874
Nickens, Eliza & al	Dilworth, Thomas	75	526	B & S	4	15	1880	4	7	1885
Nickens, James & ux	White, Chas M. tee	77	280	Trust	10	15	1886	10	23	1886
Nickens, Reuben & ux	Wilson, Stephen H.	77	426	B & S	3	4	1886	1	19	1887
Nickens, Eliza J	Russell, Mark	78	301	B & S	9	26	1887	9	26	1887
Nickens, Eliza J.	Tees W. P. B & L Asso	84	236	Trust	11	14	1893	11	14	1893
Nickens, Eliza J.	Horner, Richard R.	86	182	B & S	10	15	1894	7	1	1895
Nickens, Jennie & James	Tees C B & L Asso	87	118	Trust	4	25	1896	5	12	1896
Nickens, Eliza J .& al	Tees W P. B & L Asso	90	246	Trust	2	1	1899	3	7	1899
Nickens, Sally	Jackson, Sterling F.	90	494	B & S	7	18	1899	7	27	1899
Nickens, J M	Turner, E S Tee	96	418	Trust	Mch 27		1905	Mch 29		1905
Nickens, Mack &ux	Hipkins, Bawd D: Jno F:H B	97	465	B & S	Jan.	67	1906	Jan 30		1906
Nickens, J M	White, C M tee	101	174	Trust	Jun 20		1908	Jun 20		1908
Nickens, J M	White, C M tee	102	450	Trust	Sep 17		1909	Sep 18		1909
Nickens, John C &ux	Hurst, Nat han	106	322	B & S	Dec	1	1911	Jan	2	1912

[Above] Land deed of Nickens ancestors.

[Below] Fauquier County Register.

INDEX TO NAMES
IN ABSTRACTS OF FAUQUIER COUNTY COURT MINUTE BOOKS

NICKENS

Eliza		free person of color	Register	August 1829	p. 30
Elizabeth	age 18		Certificate of Freedom	August 1812	p. 9
Ephraim		free person of color	Register	May 1837	p. 39
Harry		free Negro	Delinquent Taxes	May 1837	p. 39
Hedgeman		free person of color	Register	November 1854	p. 67
Henrietta			Register	November 1856	p. 72
James			Certificate of Freedom	August 1805	p. 5
James	age about 5	free boy of color	OP Indenture	November 1831	p. 31
James		free boy of color	OP Indenture Rescinded	November 1831	p. 31
James	Deceased Estate	Administration granted to Wm. Nickens		April 1836	p. 36
Margaret			Register	November 1856	p. 72
Sarah			Certificate of Freedom	April 1806	p. 5

Appendix Two

Revolution War Records

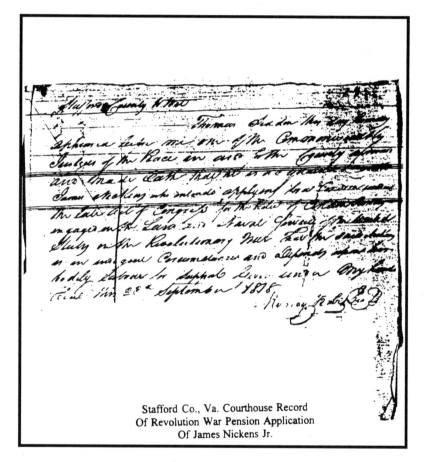

Stafford Co., Va. Courthouse Record
Of Revolution War Pension Application
Of James Nickens Jr.

Revoluntion War pension application of James Nickens, Jr.

Original application for Revolution War Pension of James Nickens, Jr.

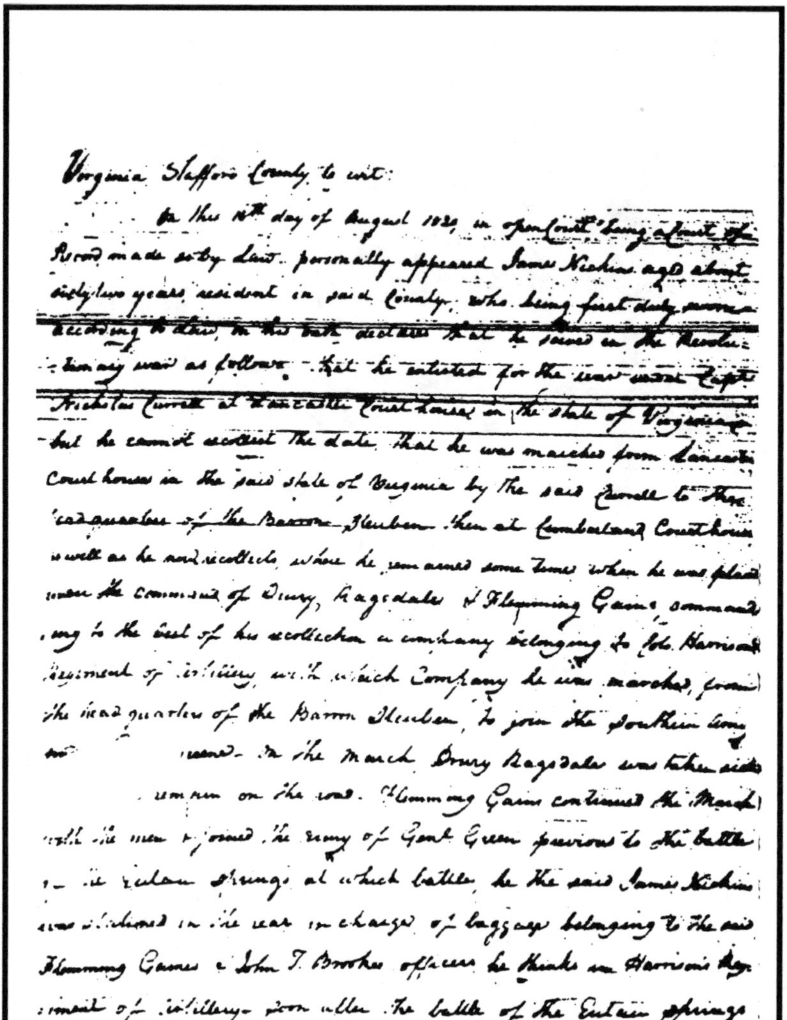

Virginia Stafford County to wit:

On this 18th day of August 1820 in open Court being a Court of Record made so by law personally appeared James Nickens aged about sixty two years resident in said County who being first duly sworn according to law, on his oath declares that he served in the Revolu-tionary war as follows - that he enlisted for the war under Capt. Nicholas Currell at Lancaster Court house in the State of Virginia but he cannot recollect the date. That he was marched from Lancaster Court house in the said state of Virginia by the said Currell to the headquarters of the Baron Steuben then at Cumberland Court house as well as he now recollects, where he remained some time when he was placed under the command of Drury Ragsdale & Flemming Gaines command-ing to the best of his recollection a company belonging to Col. Harrison's Regiment of Artillery with which Company he was marched from the head quarters of the Baron Steuben to join the Southern army [illegible] ward - On the march Drury Ragsdale was taken sick [illegible] remain on the road. Flemming Gaines continued the March with the men & joined the army of Genl Green previous to the battle of the Eutaw Springs at which battle he the said James Nickens was stationed in the rear in charge of baggage belonging to the said Flemming Gaines & John T. Brooke officers he thinks in Harrison's Reg-iment of Artillery - soon after the battle of the Eutaw Springs Drury Ragsdale resumed his command with whom he the said Nickens continued until the close of the war - when he returned with

Revolution War record of James Nickens.

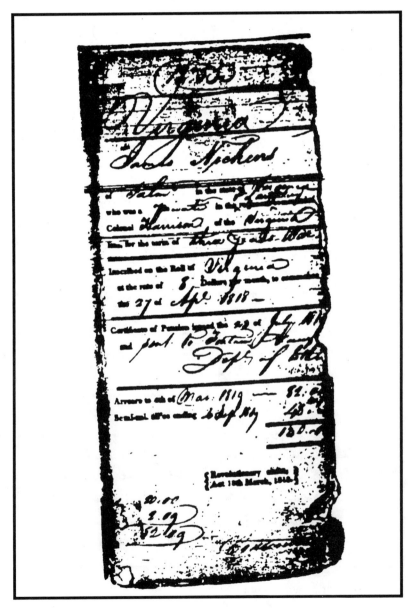

Revolution War pension certificate of James Nickens, Jr.

Appendix Three

Fauquier County Virginia
Register of Free Negroes
1817-1865

Fauquier County Virginia
Register of Free Negroes
1817-1865

-473-

NAME: Sarah Ann Nickins
AGE: About 20 years
STATURE: 5 feet high
COLOUR: Bright Mulatto
DESCRIPTION: No marks on the face, except a small mole above
               the left eye. A scar on the middle finger of the
               left hand. Black eyes, regular features, good
               teeth, hair long and inclined to curl
HOW FREE: Born Free

(Certified 24 July 1848. Copy delivered 24 July 1848.)

Freedom Paper of my great grandmother, Sally Nickens.

Contributed by Miss Daphne Gentry
Richmond, Virginia

This List of Recruits Raised in Lancaster County, Agreeable to an Act of Assembly for Recruiting this States Quota of Troops to serve in the Continental army, March 10th 1781, is filed in the Auditor's Office, Assessment Accounts, 1780-1781, at the Virginia State Library.

James Carter, Lancaster, planter, for 18 months; bounty $4000. Drafted.

Benjamin Wood, Jersies, farmer; 5 feet 4 inches high, sallow complexion, 22 years old; for the war; bounty $12000. Enlisted.

Robert Christian, Lancaster, planter; 5 feet 6 inches high, ruddy complexion, 18 years old; for 3 years; bounty $8000. Enlisted.

Mordecai Levy, Lancaster, waggoner; 5 feet 1 inch high, tawney complexion, 19 years old; for the war; bounty $12000. Enlisted.

William Cornelius, Lancaster, shoe maker: 5 feet 8 inches high, ruddy complexion, 28 years old; for 18 months; bounty $4000. Substitute.

William Norman, Lancaster, planter; 5 feet 4 inches high, brown complexion; for 18 months; bounty $4000. Substitute.

William Brumbley, Lancaster, planter; 48 years old; for 18 months; bounty $4000. Drafted.

Robert Nicken, Lancaster, planter; 5 feet 7 inches high, dark complexion, 18 years old; for 18 months; bounty $4000. Substitute.

James Nicken, Lancaster, planter; 5 feet 2 inches high, dark complexion, 17 years old; for the war; bounty $12000. Substitute.

John Monoghon, Pennsylvania, weaver; 5 feet 8 inches, light hair, ruddy complexion, 19 years old; for the war; bounty $12000. Enlisted.

Samuel Cornelius, Lancaster, drummer; 5 feet, ruddy complexion, 19 years old; for 18 months; bounty $4000. Substitute.

Richard Yerby, Lancaster, planter; 5 feet 7 inches high, ruddy complexion, 19 years old; for 18 months; bounty $4000. Drafted.

George Clutton, Lancaster, planter; 5 feet 6 inches

James Nickens, my ancestor's name is the fifth name from bottom of list.

6.

August 28th
1882

My Dear Bell

I wrote you some time ago in reference to Jennie Nickens property but receiving no reply I concluded to write again, as it is a matter of considerable impor. tance that you should understand the case in order that your niece Nannie may be protect. ed in her rights under The Law. You may not know perhaps that Nannie has an equal right in all the proper with yourself which Jennie left, after her debts are paid, and

A letter written by my great grandmother, Sallie Nickens, on behalf of a relative.

best chairs to furnish ~~Belle & Nickens~~
a room. You must also
inform Mary that the life
interest in the House is
hers only, during her life,
that it returns to ~~you if~~
~~you have after removing~~
and if ~~Mary~~ are not living
and Nonnie is, that
it goes to Nonnie at
her death — There are
two Trunks in the House
if you dont want both
of them, I should be
glad to get one.
~~Please answer this~~
at once and tell me
if you understand the
case, for it is import
ant that you should,
as I said before in order
to protect Nonnies interest
which Mary does not recog
nise at present. *Sallie Nickens*

Bibliography

Berlin, Ira. *Slaves Without Masters*. New York: Pantheon, 1974.

Birmingham, Stephen. *Certain People, America's Black Elite*. Boston, Toronto: Little Brown & Co., 1977.

Breen, T. H., and Innes, Stephen. *Myne Owne Ground; Race and Freedom in Virginia Eastern Shores, 1640-1676*. New York: Oxford Press, 1980.

Featherston. *Skin Deep*. Freedom, California: The Crossing Press, 1994.

Fergusson, J.W. *Negro Marriage and Births, 1721-1779*. Richmond, Virginia: NNA Publisher.

Fitzpatrick, Sandra, and Goodman, Maria R. *The Guide to Black Washington*. New York, N.Y.: Hippocrene Books, 1990.

Franklin, John Hope, and Moss, Jr., Alfred. *From Slavery to Freedom: A History of Negro Americans*. 6th ed. New York: Knopf, 1988.

Frazier, E. Franklin. *The Negro Family in the United States*. The Univ. of Chicago Press, 1969.

Harley, Sharon; Middleton, Stephen, and Stokes, Charlotte. *The African American Experience*. Englewood, N.J.: Globe Book Co., 1992.

Higgenbotham, A. Leon, Jr. *In Matter of Color*. Oxford Univ. Press, 1980.

Hundley, Mary Gibson. *The Dunbar Story 1850-1950*. New York, N.Y.: Vantage Press, Inc., 1905.

Jackson, Luther. "Free Negroes in Petersburgh Virginia," *Negro History*, XII.

Jernegan, Marcus. *Laboring and Dependent Classes in Colonial America - 1607-1783*. Westport, Conn.: Greenwood Press, 1931.

Kaplan, Sidney. *The Black Presence in the American Revolution*. Washington, D.C., 1973.

Lewis, Steven. *Undaunted Courage*. Manassas, Va. Manassas Museum, 1994.

Madden, T.O., with Miller, Ann L. *We Were Always Free*. New York, N.Y.: W. W. Norton & Co. Ins., 1992.

Majors, Gerri. *Black Society*. Chicago: Johnson Publishing Co. Inc., 1976.

McGinnis, Carl. *Virginia Genealogy Sources and Resources*.

Morgan, Edmund S. *American Slavery, American Freedom: The Ordeal of Colonial Virginia*. New York: W. W. Norton, 1975.

National Archives. Washington, D.C.: Publications Sales Branch (NEPS).

Quarles, Benjamin. *The Negro in the Making of America*. New York: Oxford Univ. Press, 1977.

Roundtree, Helen. *Pocohantas People*. Norman, Oklahoma. Oklahoma Univ.

Russel, John H. *The Free Negro in Virginia, 1617-1865*. Baltimore, Md.: Johns Hopkins Press, 1913.

Sutton, Karen. *The Nickens Family: Tracing Non-Slave African Americans*. A Genealogy Genogram, 1994.

Wheeler, Anthony. *Evolution of a Southern Tidewater Community - Lancaster, Virginia 1650-1750*.

Order Form

Postal orders:

HonocanPress

P.O. Box 240
5856 College Avenue
Oakland CA 94618
USA

Please send ____ copies of Carry Me Back.

Name: _____

Address: _____

City: _____State: _____ Zip: _____-_____

Telephone:_____Fax:_____

E-mail address_____

Quantity Discounts Available.

Please enclose $17.95 (check or money order)
- Sales tax: Please add 8.25% for books shipped to California addresses. ($19.43 total per book)
- Shipping: $3.00 for first book and $2.00 for each additional book

Payment: Check_____ Money Order_____
Please make payable to Honocan Press.